Bert Widman

AF271996

The Stone Age Of Faith

An evolutionary farewell to churches and sects.

In plain language.

In ecclesias

O. A. M. D. G.

„Just as the heart can live in love only, so does the spirit in the striving for insight and truth. In the middle of tempestous times, during the daily work, among all oppressions and vileness one should lift the gaze freely and boldly towards the splendour of heaven and try to grasp and fathom the very origin of truth and beauty, one´s own spirit, the spiritual harvest of man in all centuries and the nature surrounding us. One should always keep in mind, however, that only humbleness brings greatness and that all wisdom and insight serve only those who live and act accordingly.“

Cardinal Nikolaus Cusanus, 1453

„To accept that absolute truth is beyond the grasp of man is the beginning of all tolerance and the antidote against all ideologies. The insight that we are parts and passing witnesses of a history that is unfolding since billionS of years in the cosmos, producing orders of ever increasing complexity and beauty and which, at the same time, transcends the grasp of human understanding forever - this is the begin of all religiousness.“

Professor Hoimar von Ditfurth
in his acceptance speech of the
UNESCO Kalinga Prize, 1980

There is no need to predict the future, but to be prepared for it.

Perikles (?)

LIST OF CONTENTS

LIST OF CONTENTS (CTD)

INTRODUCTION

Walter and I are old friends. Over the years we found sheer spiritual pleasure in our discussions on „God And The World", as we smilingly called them. We soon found out, however, that we had to apply more method to them and that we had to do a lot of homework. So we did this for decades with ever increasing pleasure.

We followed the riverbeds of human consciousness through the milleniums. We saw how streams of thought developed, parted and united. We saw them becoming stale waters of doctrine and dogma, how they turned into torrents or evaporated in the desert of some theology.

During the years we concentrated on the great minds, from Democrit to Shankara and many others, up to Mahatma Ghandi and Teilhard de Chardin. We literally fought with ever increasing distaste through the so-called Old Testament. We found Paul to be the ultimate source of the travesty that usurped the revelation.

We bowed before the natural scientists of the last centuries, being the true heralds of evolution in the face of oppressive churches, from Galilee, Bruno, Kopernik, Kepler, Newton up to Darwin and Spencer.

And parallel to that we developed an ever increasing inner furor on the seas of blood and tears which spilled since 5.000 years from the unholy fraternizing between priest-run churches and state systems.

We studied the history of Islam very carefully. We bow to the Mutazilites and to the great philosophers in the Middle Ages. Besides the Koran we also read with reverence and spiritual profit the Baghavad-Gita.

When asked as to whom we owe most in our feeding period of some thirty years we do not hesitate to name Will and Ariel Durant, the last pair of writers who were able to produce an integrated cultural history of mankind, a gigantic and life-consuming task. We still drink with great gusto from their well, starting again with the first volume after having closed their last.

Above every man and thing, however, we saw the revelation of the one Divine Power to this unimportant planet, coming through the man Yeshua roughly 2.000 years ago. In this we see the ultimate evolutionary standard which is slowly, too slowly coming into the focus of searching man.

We know from the Logos in Yeshua that the Creator is shaping the universe by evolution. At the same time, however, we have to state that this message from Yeshua has not been accepted by the great religions, not by the so so-called „christian" ones nor is there an evolutionary understanding of their deity in the Islam or in the Hebrew faith.

Walter and I agree that it was the natural sciences who pushed open one window after another during the past 400 years. They have paved the road towards a breathtaking terrestrial and cosmic scenery, the evolution of matter as well as that of consciousness. We owe the insight to them, not to the religious communities, that evolution is a cosmic principle or rather, the cosmic principle i s evolution. We felt sorry for the Nobel laureate who answered „Of course not, I am a scientist" when being asked whether he believed in a God, or for Laplace who answered Napoleon´s similar question with his famous „I had no need for this hypothesis".

Nowhere could we register that the power of creation should feel „crowded in" by the sciences - if this human phrase is excused - when one square after another of the scientific grid system is lighted up - quite on the contrary! The more we participate in how the natural sciences are pushing forward to the outmost boundaries of the universe and into the innermost realms of matter, the greater becomes our wondrous respect before this Divine Power which penetrates, moves and encompasses anything in this cosmos.

Our unimportant planet as the center of the universe? We are able to smile at this notion but only because Galilee, Bruno, Kopernik and Kepler literally dared their life in order to show proof to the contrary.

To have our planet, however, as the singular place of a revelation when a critical mass of consciousness had developed on it - this still is the incredible hyperbole of all religious communities in this world today. It is not easy to smile on this conceited notion, especially after having heard the contrary from the power of creation, speaking out of Yeshua.

With that we have come to the focal point of this long, perhaps too long, introduction. This book will be nothing less than an expedition that starts with good equipment but also with a lot of ballast. This is why we grouped the contents into the three chapters:

1.   Ballast

Our faith in the essence of the revelation through Yeshua is weighted down by so many an empty vessel whose contents have evaporated with an ever increasing evolutionary consciousness. The vessels, however, are still standing on the wagon, as ordered by the priest churches. In order to remain short we could not lift the lid of every one, only of those which appeared especially unwieldy.

2.   Space Probes

Stemming from our belief that the revelation out of Yeshua is definitely evolutionary we tried in the second chapter to push the horizons well over those of the churches. We believe that our planet cannot be seen as a singular or unique case of a revelation, but is imbedded in this cosmic development with countless others which have long ago produced reflexive consciousness, „contemporary" with us or in future eons. We tried to find some intelligent and trustful assumptions with our space probes, as we called them. Some of them have given us deep satisfaction.

3.   Direction

Also in the last chapter we wanted to put honesty before speculation when discussing justified probabilities of the future development of human consciousness. We are convinced that the general direction of the evolution of the religious mind will take this approximate direction. With some points we may have jumped to conclusions but we see a high degree of probability in the described general course for the next centuries. And: if we should be wrong, there is no harm done.

First of all, Walter and I are insignificant explorers. Secondly, the evolution of our mind has practically begun one second ago, if we are putting it on a time scale of our earth´s development. And we all know that evolution has time, much time indeed, and will always start a new try while we see only dead ends.

So much for the gist of contents.

We have never been tempted to develop a new theological, theosophical or philosophical system or to found another new religious community in addition to the thousands of useless and intolerant organizations which populate our planet at present.

Still less, we did not write down our discussions for the beautiful and pious souls in order to elevate their spirits. Most of it, on the contrary, will be blasted by them as anathema, because inevitably we are drawing some comfortable pillows of faith from under their necks. We want to assure them that our intent was not to hurt or humiliate them. If they are drawing comfort and direction from their traditional beliefs we do not want to belittle them. We all arrive at the same goal finally; the difference is only the route taken and the baggage in tow.

Please bear with this introduction for another moment.
When we asked ourselves, f o r   w h o m   we should write down our discussions, Walter and I very readily agreed to the following:

- For all those who are of our opinion that the priest churches and sects of all kinds have gambled away the revelation through Yeshua, each organization in a different but many in similar manner.

- For everybody who feels that the revelation through Yeshua reaches far beyond our little planet.

- For the many, who like us, have developed a hearty distaste of the elitist mumbojumbo and infights of theologians of all centuries, especially of those in the present times.

This is why we decided to talk simply and clearly to women and men who are sick of being fed undigestable footnotes and bible citations on every page. This meant, of course, to waive „scientific claim". We gladly did so. It was important to us not to reach the professors but the worker, the farmer, the housewife, bus driver, mailman - those who have capitulated long ago before the awesome and exclusive knowledge of their priest castes. Having done so, they also refrained to read the four reports on Yeshua with a new interest.

In short: we wanted to be understandable. Keeping this in mind we discussed and wrote with a trusting simplicity and evolutionary impetus, because both of them are apt to widen the horizon of our expectations far more than any „scientific" treatise.

The patient reader is now invited to embark on our expedition, upon her or his own risk. May we assure you, however, that no risk appeared more grandiose to us than this one. May the same happen to you.

Chapter I:

BALLAST SAMPLES

Another Book On God And The World?

It was a spring Sunday. Walter and I were sitting on a hilltop in the morning, gazing gratefully at the morning sun, the Alps and the lake below us.

W: Do you hear the church bells down in the village?

B: Yes. In five minutes you will hear another one, but one only. That is the bell of the Protestant church then.

W: Ringing together would be bad style, hm?

B: Sure. The protestant bell would be simply drowned. Both parish priests never had a problem there. One is considerate to the other and to his flock also.

W: Did they have an ecumenic service already, down there?

B: Once a year they do, not more often.

W: Some sort of alibi performance?

B: You may call it that.

W: I can well imagine what is ticking in the heads of the two sheperds down there. They would like to hold joint services much more often, but they are captives of their systems. There is the Church Board, the deacon, the bishop and so on until we arrive at the Vatican or at the Lutheran World Conference - no chance.

B: So it happens when priests are paid officials. Who is paying calls the tune and an unperturbed sense of duty is rated much higher than risky ecumenical embraces.

W: The Lutheran pastor has to feed a family. Would you be foolhardy enough to risk bread and pension just because of a few ecumenical services more per year? The same problem is with the catholic priest: he learnt nothing but theology. Bread goes before strong convictions, let alone weaker ones.

B: It´s not a new problem. The priest hierarchy of Egypt and Babylon surely whipped their officials into order much more harsher. Only the quality of the risk of life has changed since then.

W: I think the problem goes far deeper. Call it priest caste or church organization, as you like, the signals to the individual are the same since milleniums: God can be found only in their system and only by those who obey to the rules and rites. Only then God will listen to him and „God help" those who are trying to sidestep them. Nowadays you are not burned for that any more, but they are locking eternity carefully for you, because they are administering the keys to kingdom and are keepers of the lone truth; each church, each sect, very exclusively.

B: Are you astonished by that? The secular powers over five thousand years recognized very acutely the instrument of dominance that is formed by the pacts of zealous faith organizations combined with their own arsenal. Together they formed a system without escape; adversary of the religious organization - enemy of the state, and vice versa. The faith itself was forever the loser in this power play.

W: It´s good that we are away already since a few hundred years from the danger that religious organizations could call on the unquestioning help of the secular arm in order to punish disbelievers. The unholy alliance of throne and altar is a matter of the past.

B: I disagree. The so-called Christian churches have degenerated into adapting organizations, especially the Catholic one. Upholding the system is their foremost concern. In order to succeed in that they need a benign state. In order to stabilize the cooperation they even sacrifice millimeters of their doctrine in order to be in basic unison with constitution and laws. The underlying rationale, however, has been always the same: any authority comes from God, as you can read in the letters of Paul and Peter. And silently these organizations are adding: and we are the only ones who know what God wants.

W: My view of the total problem is a little more complex. The so-called Christian beliefs have not only separated from their believers by fraternizing with the secular powers. They also have reached a state of aloofness, I mean: they have been carried away, upwards.

B: How is that?

W: Priests do not talk to the people in comprehensible terms any more, but preach and write for or against each other in the first line, very scientific of course, but in a language that is not understood any more by a mailman, bus driver, farmer or housewife - practically by nobody without higher education or having studied philosophy or theology - and I doubt if that would help.

B: And what is the lesson of history?

W: I just wanted to come round to that. Wherever we look back religious systems started to die when their ruling class chose to speak in an elitist language to which the believers had no access to. Mostly this was premeditated; the people should not find access to the rites, mysteria and language in order to preserve the unquestioned role of the only gate to the gods: the priests.

B: Would you say that the priest churches of today are emulating this?

W: I could offer a long string of names now, famous within their churches, who are churning out elaborate volumes every second year on fundamental or refined aspects of faith. Whom do they reach? The bus driver, housewife, farmer? None of them. But as long as somebody pays for their meals they will go on doing so.

The so-called christian churches are ruled by thinkers in splendid ivory towers on one side, on the other by managers who are running Church Incorporated. They represent the churches, not the believers. I think that there is hardly any difference in the Shinto system.

B: But there was a Mother Teresa -

W: A great woman, no doubt, but also a very welcome alibi figure for the organization.

B: To sum it up: we are pronouncing the death of the so-called christian churches. But they are dying of more than one cause, isn´t it? Not to be understood by most of their believers may not lead to sudden asphyxiation -

W: I propose that we strike out the word „sudden" in our discussion. We are facing an evolutionary development where sudden occurrences just do not happen. But what we are witnessing here is the protracted agony of the so-called christian organizations. In spite of all power and splendour that came to them over the centuries the seeds of their destruction have been laid at their very beginning as organizations. The first poison that crept into the organism was that they very soon were putting the organization over faith. Having become new centres of power in the declining Roman empire, East and West, they offered themselves as welcome administrative structures who were able and willing to perform political tasks - and were slowly but surely corrupted by them.

B: I agree. The second bazillus in my opinion is that the revelation of God through the Nazarene Yeshua was very soon turned into an elitist „science", theology. You could say it started with the so-called Church Fathers, carried on by the prolific Augustine and culminating in the hyperbole of the Scholastics.

It is ridiculous, if it were not so tragic, to see how they tried to pull God under the microscope of our limited perception in order to become nearer to his being by the categories of biology, space, time, cause and effect -

W: But isn´t research legitimate? All progress is derived from it?

B: Of course, up to a definite point only, which Newton expressed in his „hypotheses non fingo - I do not dream up hypotheses", when he was asked why gravit y existed. Theology however, the „science of God", consists of little else than hypotheses constructed by a state of mind which is, in evolutionary terms, embryonic at best.

Whatever seemed plausible to our three-dimensional mind and two genders was elevated to infallible truth by congregations of old men - women never had a voice in councils, Paul saw to that - and disbelievers were simply killed in order to restore peace.

W: Theology as a science, this is not the curse. The fact however, that it became an intransigent, intolerant science, suppressing the natural sciences just as ruthlessly as philosophical thinking, this became the poison. They are trying to cure the body nowadays, but the damage inflicted on human consciousness, trust and tolerance is irreparable.

B: So it is. But the main symptom is still rampant: only somebody who has passed their exams in theology is entitled to participate in a discussion on God And The World.

W: I am smiling every time I hear a Pope calling out to other faiths in the world to enter into a dialogue.

B: Let us go on in our diagnosis. In my opinion one more cause of death among the so-called christian churches is their blatant disregard of human life, human misery. I get physically sick when I read about their crusades against birth control and making themselves the guardians of untouchable life. At these moments I see the horror scenarios of the Crusades, the inquisition, the genocide in Latin America, the slave trade, the witch hunts, and ultimately the holocaust of the Jews - all this was possible only because the so-called christian churches were either the instigators or just looked the other way. They have forfeited forever the right to speak for protection of life. In fact, they have committed high treason on the revelation coming through Yeshua, that knows the elementary commandment to love your fellow man.

W: I have read „The Criminal History Of Christendom" also, plus some other publications. They are all well researched, no church was ever able to discredit them on historical grounds. But let´s face it: wasn´t much of it excusable? Haven´t many cruelties been committed under a burning dedication for the cause of God? Were they not offsprings of cruel ages where human life counted very little anyway?

B: I have heard this sort of excuse often enough and it nauseates me. My answer is: No! Organizations who base themselves on the revelation through Yeshua, who earnestly believe that the Holy Spirit has been farmed out to them exclusively, they have committed the unforgivable sin against just this Spirit, which can be done also by an organization, not only by natural persons. No! These churches may thank Paul, the Scholastics, the Dominicans and Jesuits for that.

The „burning dedication for God´s cause", as you expressed it so graciously, was in most cases ruthless support for dynasties and their spoils of occupation and exploitation, of which a good percentage always found its way into the organization coffers. Ultimately all this served to bolster the power of the organization and was accomplished literally over mountains of corpses and seas of tears and blood.

I am going one step further: the surging of socialism and communism as an action in despair by people who were exploited by thrones and altars alike is the direct result of the neglect which the churches showed to human misery at all times.

W: But communism could not change that either, as we see today?

B: Correct, but why not? Because their leaders only saw the external symptoms of the systems which they wanted to abolish, but not the real causes, who caught up with them in no time. Very soon you could not find a basic difference of their structures and those of the churches: Commanded articles of faith, extermination of dissenters, loss of private liberties, witch hunts that ended in psychiatric wards here, not on the stake, and above all an omnipotent power central with infallible Central Committees. One should not wonder, therefore.

W: I should like to bring in a last deadly bazillus. It is well outside the sphere of human error or depravity; it is rooted again in theology: it is the impotence of the great religions of these days to think in evolutionary terms. The so-called christian religions but also the Islam and the Hebrew religion have each deposited their thoughts and commanded truths nicely in a safe vault each. More must not go into it and nothing must be taken out of it, otherwise the total contents would be jeopardized.

It is of no importance to the vaults that the natural sciences have acknowledged evolution as a secured component of human understanding, having gotten rid of their janitors after centuries.

The vaults are also not disturbed by the fact that we have realized already that evolutionary processes on our unimportant tiny planet are occurring in the whole observable cosmos as a universal principle. Because this is happening around us and over our heads we have to give new thought also to many parts of the reports on Yeshua, to recognize the evolutionary content in them and to realize the explosive capacity that will tear the vaults apart.

Or, let it put me in another way: the God of the three great religions has been dimensioned by them too humanly and far too small. This is why they suffer from malnutrition and anemia. They have become unable for self-renewal. With that, they have condemned themselves to death before an evolutionary tide that will wash them away. They do not need executioners, they are dying from their own hand: so-called Christianity, the Islam and the Hebrew religion, not to speak of the hundreds of bizarre sects in their trail.

B: I agree. There is an example in simple biology: organismsthat have developed an outer hard shell, as e.g. many insects, are unable to evolve into bigger organisms. The shells, the vaults - the same. So what do we cry now? „The churches are dead, long live the faith!" Or what?

W: I want to be very precise here: long live the faith in the one Divine Power who has spoken to us through the man Yeshua, in the evolutionary aspect of the reports on him.

B: Something else now. We are discussing these things now for years and we have done our homework quite thoroughly, I should say. Today for instance we have brought some things into good focus within a short time. What do you think about writing down our discussions and have them published?

W: What a nonsense! The books who have been written about „God And The World", if laid on top of each other, probably reach from here to the moon.

B: That may be. But how many of them have been read by your mailmain, bus driver, housewife next door? Ninety nine percent of all these books is elitist „scientific" writing, carrying fifteen footnotes on each page. Without citing bible phrases or taking reinsurance in something written before nobody dares to write about God any more!

W: You want to write a book about God without taking recourse to bible sentences, theologians or canonized saints? You are mad!

B: I do not think that your remark was very evolutionary. I am not thinking either of yet another broadside into the churches and sects, not that. I am thinking of the future, of an approximation to the revelation given through Yeshua in evolutionary thinking. I concede without argument that our evolutionary horizon is modest, to say the least; we would be on our limits quite fast, I suppose.

W: And then you take resort to „intelligent" assumptions. Finally you will end up in christian or theosophic science fiction.

B: Your doubts are richly deserved. But believe me: it should be far from us to delve in mystic ruminations, no. One would have to look for very concrete guideposts all the way, rules of the game, so to say, or call it simply self-discipline. Only then such a book would become digestible for the readers we have in mind. Only then they would not throw it into the waste basket after a few pages.

W: You mean that it must be thrilling?

B: That would certainly help. But not like a mystery novel, where you find the solution on the last pages, more like an expedition report. It would be thrilling enough.

W: An expedition into the Uncertain Unknown?

B: Exactly the opposite: a travel of thought to evolutionary shores of which we see the hazy outlines only at present.

W: Discovery of new shores?

B: In our perception of the revelation, maybe, but not a new message. We trust this message because we feel that its basic content is evolutionary. It only needs a little courage to see it that way. Religious organizations never felt the need to try it.

W: Do you think in earnest that such a manuscript would find a publisher? Crazy idea!

B: I do not know. Maybe he would have to be just a little bit crazy also in the way we are. Incompetence or crazyness would be the nicer expressions which will be hurled at us - and him. The whole establishment would fall on us, i.e., if they condescend to do so. More probable is that the printed book would receive benign neglect - not to be taken seriously, a non-scientific elaborate by laymen. Finis.

W: Maybe it would become a footnote some day in their books?

B: Not even that. You may have the unpublished manuscript placed on your belly in the coffin. It would look great! But, jokes aside now: are you having the courage to write this book with me or not?

W: You have an evil manner to rouse my interest and opposition at the same time. What am I going for? All right, we do it.

CHOSEN PEOPLE?

Evidently we had to include the so-called Old Testament in our discussions. As a result we do not see these scripts as a pre-condition or fertile ground for the revelation through Yeshua, from which it should proceed by inner necessity. Quite to the contrary!

We see in it the unsuccessful and consequently aborted try by the Divine Power to unfold her revelation on this planet via this little ethnic group. Their tribes believed, after myths and polytheism, to have found a deity, or having been singled out by her, who was willing to enter into an exclusive contract. Upholding the contract consisted of venerating this openly jealous deity as the sole God and to subordinate government, social system and land robbery to her exclusively. In this quid pro quo the contract price came always swiftly, so did the penalties; subjugating and murdering other tribes or being subjugated and murdered by bigger powers. This treaty lasted for a long time; in their minds it was still in force during the captivity in Babylon and was steadfastly adhered to even when Israel had long since been degraded to a Roman province. In these political nadir points the belief was most fervent: that they are not one, but t h e chosen people and that Israel, assisted by their deity, would move up to political world dominance.

The evolution of the mind, or the original revelation, if there ever was one, went overboard long ago in this play, suffocated by delusions of grandeur and cemented by 613 ritual laws. The perennial anxiety to step outside of this sacred circle consequently produced the concept of „sin".

So: a reactor accident at some point in the development of human consciousness? The reader is invited to listen to our discussion:

W: First of all, I think, we have to discuss the basic question how the Divine Power would or could reveal herself on this planet -

B: Objection! If we put the question this way we would open the door widely to the cardinal mistake of the theologians, namely, to calibrate our infinitesimal small power of conception to be the measure of all things. O n e thesis we have admitted long ago: only the existence of reflexive thinking makes living beings prepared for receiving the revelation. We cannot communicate with an amoeba nor can the

Divine Power reveal herself to one. If you, however, are putting the question in what way only the Divine Power could manifest herself on this planet then we are thrown back immediately into the theological hyperbole of probing God´s mind by time, space and cause-effect.

W: All right. I strike out the word „could". It is permissible then to think about the „would"?

B: If we do not imagine to probe the will of the Divine Power, yes.

W: Then we are left with assumptions only?

B: We have little else; but also assumptions can be very far-reaching sometimes.

W: Then let me start again: we assume that the Divine Power saw an evolutionary basis on this planet for her revelation -

B: Excuse me for interrupting you once again. Don´t you think we should clarify first what „revelation" means in our terms?

W: Apparently this is your critical day today. „Revelation" is nothing else than the message to reflexive minds by the Divine Power that she exists. Secondly, that she is not viewing us indifferently but that she offers to share a spiritual existence with her after one´s bodily life. Thirdly: that this offer is not to be had for nothing. We, in this case, have to develop the spirit-forming attitudes while we still have a material body - or at least give it an honest try. In short: God is, God cares, God gives, God wants.

B: Beautifully formulated! Carry on!

W: Without interruption now?

B: How should I know? We are not delivering lectures, do we, but are discussing.

W: There is the assumption, therefore, that the Divine Power chose not to introduce her revelation on this planet with an act of power, before which the human mind collapsed in terror, lightning-swift and with unimaginable force and beauty. We know that it did not happen this way. But: why not?

B: Alas, why not? With that more than 10.000 terrestrial years could have been evaded, full of terror, blood and tears.

W: I think that it is connected to the concept of free will. The philosophers of all centuries have filled libraries with their notions that our species has a free will or has not. Same as with the arguments that man is evil or good by nature. Now, anybody who has read a little on biological evolution knows today that our behaviour is still largely governed by the inherited behaviour of our species, which haunts us since millions of years, having us helped to survive before that.

Our will has a history, therefore, the history of the victor who managed to preserve and proliferate his kind, very clearly to the detriment or extinction of others.

B: Has the victor now a free will or not?

W: He/she has it to the extent that he/she manages to extricate him- or herself-form the hereditary behaviour of our species. Mr. von Ditfurth would say: to the extent that our cranium with its powers of reflexive thinking is able to control the older brain formations.

B: Has our species arrived at this point already?

W: You know very well that this is not the case by far! This you are noticing every time when you become afraid or get angry. We all notice this if once again an ethnic group is butchering another one, with all technical perfection. You just have to look to Ruanda and to the Balkans.

B: So practically there is not yet free will, or what?

W: Surely there is. Who is not afraid any more, who is not rising in sudden anger, who is opposing genocide, that will is free, because it has thrown off the mortgages of primeval behaviour. Certainly one does not arrive at this state suddenly, more so stumbling, but - with free will.

B: Have you arrived there already?

W: No, but I try to, and within this effort I have my own free will already active. Do you feel differently?

B: No.

W: I know that you will attack the following, but nevertheless: The gradual awakening of reflexive consciousness in our species was not yet a sufficient basis for a revelation of the Divine Power. Only as we began to form social structures, to create laws which should make life bearable with one another, or to put it simply: when we were developed enough to create rules of behaviour contrary to those who governed our primate brains, then we were ripe for the revelation, because the collective and individual mind wanted the installation of a human order.

B: You wanted to say that first a certain inclination to ethical behaviour had to be there in order to make us eligible for the revelation?

W: I notice acutely in what direction you want to mislead me. With that you wanted to say that the Divine Power has consistently bypassed highly ethical cultures of the ancient world, not giving one of them her revelation? We agree that the revelation of the Divine Power is not something that „comes" to a habitat of free will but has been there since the creation of the universe, part and parcel of cosmic evolution. Habitats are growing into the revelation which surrounds them. We shall discuss more of this in the second chapter, we have agreed.

B: But the Divine Power had to make a choice, isn´t it? The Hebrew claim that they were chosen, and only they.

W: We have only their word for it.

B: And the scriptures of this people?

W: Ah, the scriptures! If you are of the opinion that they are God´s words or will, which is everybody´s privilege, then you have decided to board the direct train that takes you to Judaic Christianity, Old and New Testament being the celestial pillars of faith, because they are God´s words. It is a very easy ride, I grant you that, with an inescapable intrinsic logic - once you belief in the presence of the „Holy Spirit" in the so-called Old Testament.

B: Markion was silenced very quickly with his dissenting notions.

W: Thousands have stood up for him, so do we. The so-called Old Testament is wonderful tribal history, written by the victor. The scripts carry all the human attributes of their leading characters, making them colorful, tight and almost touchable. There are Abraham, Moses, Saul, David, Solomon, also the butchers Gideon and Josua. There are the heart-gripping tales on Ruth, Esther or Judith.

The historical truth of all this tribal history has been vindicated by archeology during the last hundredandfifty years. There the bible is right. But right in what? That certain leaders really existed? That cities having definite names were on definite locations? That this tribal history has its intrinsic, if warped, logic? All this is immaterial!

B: What is material then, please?

W: The fact that this ethnic group claimed to have received the revelation of the Divine Power, which it clearly did not.

B: How can you say such a thing?

W: Because God, as we both believe in him, does not an about-face in his basic intentions within 3.000 terrestrial years.

B: Would you care to explain?

W: Certainly I would care. Here we are at the fundamental point: The God of the so-called Old Testament is not the Divine Power that spoke through Yeshua. And it was this Logos from Yeshua who clearly told them so. If the essence of the revelation through Yeshua would have been imparted to the Hebrews 2.000 years before his appearance then the total development would have taken another direction.

That leaves us with two choices. One is that the first revelation was given exactly as later through Yeshua. If so, this ethnic group made a singular perversion of it. If so, they never came near to the essence of the revelation. Orders to eradicate other tribes or cities were very well understood, on the other hand. They formed their deity - the word God is out of place in this context - to a perfect instrument: endowed with all the features of a wily beduin chieftain, as Egon Friedell aptly remarked, unforgiving, merciless, jealous, subject to moods and above all a deity which could be offended and which really was offended. A very practical deity, in fact, very useful to instal religious and social discipline, administered by a priest caste. Naked power politics could be justified as a service to the Almighty, something that evokes strange echoes from younger and European history.

B: Stop for a moment here, please! You are still in field no. 1, that you labeled „Perverted Revelation". Correct?

W: So it is.

B: And what is your field no. 2 then?

W: No revelation at all. It just did not happen. Their deity was taken from the arsenal of Kanaanite gods, one of whom was Yahu, later Jahve. The fact that the Ten Commandments demanded adherence to one god only never has been a substitute for a revelation as it came through Yeshua. In fact, they were only the rudiments of social structure. King Hammurabi´s codex which originated roughly in the same epoch is a far more detailed, balanced and a fair code of ethics.

B: Let us be very precise about this second option. If no revelation had been given in the first place then it would be very hard to imagine that a development had taken place to which Yeshua would or could connect later on, isn´t it? But he did so!

W: Strict monotheism over centuries would also create this basis in my opinion. The spirit through Yeshua told them repeatedly that the Hebrews only thought they had an idea of the Divine Power, which they clearly had not. On the other hand, neither of the four reports on Yeshuy makes a reference to the effect that the full revelation had been entrusted to them long ago but had been perverted.

B: Could it have been a part of the revelation?

W: This piece-by-piece revelation is a well-coveted explanation by the so-called christian churches and they infer that it is highly evolutionary also. You literally find it in the protocol of Vaticanum II where they say: „... increasing according to the understanding potential of mankind". Could you imagine for a moment that the Divine Power is delivering bits and pieces of information on herself and let a tiny ethnic group develop it further by trial and error, until the need for the next portion would be evident, correcting at least half of the notions arrived at? I call this „patchwork revelation". It may have been a convenient excuse a hundred years ago, but it does not hold water before an evolutionary background.

B: I have noticed very acutely that you refer to the Hebrews as „a tiny ethnic group", more than once. I think you wanted to say that this group is not „mankind" or representing mankind in any respect at their time?

W: Exactly so. It is absolutely disappointing for me that a tiny nomadic tribe should be in a position to lay claim to the exclusive revelation if you look on the peoples and systems that outshone them in civilization long before them, contemporary and after.

B: Would you care to give a few examples?

W: I try to be short, otherwise we could dedicate the whole book to this issue only. So let us see: there is the Indian culture, the Vedic era and Buddhism. Personalities like Shankara or Ashoka would have readily listened to the revelation, I suppose.

Li Lao-Tse wrote his Tao-te-ching, the „Book on the path and virtue" roughly 500 years before Yeshua entered the stage. Kung-fu-tse was only 50 years younger than Lao-Tse. Both of them, just as Buddha, had no spiritual need for the existence of a personal God. But look how their teachings influenced generations and millions.

B: Are there any scientific data on what percentage of the world population was represented by the Hebrew tribes then?

W: I do not know of such data. In my estimate it could not have been more than one percent, maximum. But I am not through yet with alternatives: we had the Greek philosophers, Demokrit, Platon, Aristoteles and we had Sokrates. Were these 500 years before the appearance of Yeshua not a unique forum for the revelation of the Divine Power?

B: Definitely, in my opinion, and much more preferable.

W: I think we have said our piece of mind. To say more would lead us to arrogance, because we would try to accuse the Divine Power of having missed the best moments of revelation.

B: Yeshua´s attitude can be understood only, however, if he holds his people responsible on the basis of a perverted revelation. If no revelation had been given, their state of consciousness may have been quite excusable.

W: I am willing to settle for this hypothesis. So it was a perverted revelation. But this invariably leads us to another aspect, rather to the question: „Does the Divine Power want to be omniscient?" We shall come back to this question serveral times in the next chapters. Here, however, we face a development that has gone afoul of the expectations. The Divine Power decides to act, speaks through Yeshua. Had he offered twelve legions of angels to wipe away the hated Romans, he could have demanded everything else from them afterwards. As we know, this was not the case. He preached them a God that was the sharp contrary of their deity and they did not want to have any of it. An omniscient Divine Power clearly would have foreseen this.

B: But it had foreseen it. The prophecies over centuries are centering just on this point of failure. And this is also the point where we are faced with a bizarre scenario: a tiny people (not mankind) will embezzle the revelation, will „sin" against God. Foreseen. To atone for this foreseen misbehaviour, this God demands a sacrifice, in order to be reconciled with mankind, remember: mankind, not one per cent thereof. But, says the deity, which we should call her better here, no sacrifice you could think of will satisfy me. The only sacrifice acceptable to me consists of the body of a man from your middle, on whom I shall send my Spirit. I foresee that you will not listen to him. I foresee that you will torture and murder him. All your sins are thrown on him, he will end in despair. But: he shall live on forever after, with me. The blood-curdling nonsense and uselessness of this reasoning is evident. Here we have not even a deity, but a creative monster that is allowing his creations to rebel but meets out punishment to one only, and this one was the carrier of his voice. Absurdity carried to the extreme!

W: This is all very moving, as you present the case. Only you overlook that Yeshua accepted this role, not willingly though, but obediently.

B: I doubt this very much. We have made a great distinction in all our discussions between Yeshua the Hebrew and the Logos of God speaking through him - of course not always and not always in the same intensity.

W: Arius would have been very proud of you!

B: I am dead earnest. Yeshua the Hebrew knew all these prophecies; he also knew that he had been selected as the Voice of God. But he chose to act out the prophetic scenario as Yeshua the Hebrew, drawing the prophecy on him. Only by this attitude the four reports on him gain an inner logic, because the way he treats the priest caste of his people can end in disaster only.

W: Pre-meditated suicide, do you mean that?

B: Pre-meditated self-immolation comes nearer to the goal.

W: And you think that there was never, at no time, any alternative?

B: Now we really are back to square one: did God not only foresee, but want this development? If he did then I am having severe problems with him. If he decided that the scenario should have an open end, then why was Yeshua under the whip?

W: Could we not put the question aside by saying that this is a mystery?

B: I definitely refuse to do that! The whole scenario is atavistic, illogical, slaps human history in other parts of the world smack in the face, reeks of human sacrifices in stone-age times and is above all inconsistent with the God that spoke out of Yeshua.

W: In the Hebrew prophets there is the prediction that the revelation will be taken from this people and be given to the pagans. What revelation could be meant by this? The one which the Hebrews received long ago and destroyed, or that which came through Yeshua?

B: The one by Yeshua, in my belief. Because there never was an exclusive contract between this handful of nomads and the Divine Power beforehand.

W: The revelation is still an open game then?

B: There has never been a scenario with a pre-ordained end for the revelation on this planet.

W: I agree. Otherwise we would be only marionettes on the strings of a cosmic puppeteer.

B: Looking on the performance of the so-called christian churches, there we have the second - or third - perversion of the revelation, isn´t it?

W: Yes. The second fiasco in my opinion.

B: How many more tries will the Divine Power accord this planet? Or is she facing us impassively like a chemist whose first and second test misfired?

W: Objection, please! It is we that have misfired and this is why I firmly believe that we shall have many more tries. Where do I draw my trust from? Because I do not see the Divine Power as the cold Chief Engineer of evolution, but as a loving force. This is why the gory scenario of redemption does not fit into this picture; this is also the reason why there will be just so many tries, and just so many carriers of the revelation, until it has transformed the minds of our habitat thoroughly, evolutionary.

B: This precludes „authorized" or „exclusive" persons and organizations by itself.

W: Very much so. The torch of revelation has been carried by the natural sciences during the past centuries. We shall see to whom it will be passed next, and these next ones will not be the last bearers.

B: How do we leave the omniscience of God in this discussion?

W: With all respect before the Divine Power, I doubt that she is interested to be omniscient in detail. She has of course a goal in mind, for the reflexive minds of all habitats in this cosmos. But this is something we want to discuss in another place in this book.

B: Will there ever be a chosen people, here or in some other habitat of the universe?

W: It would be the worst thing that could happen to a habitat. We are still in the repair phase of this unevolutionary notion.

A Son?

After our discussion in the aforegoing chapter is was evident already that we could not bypass the following „A Son?" I protested mildly, because of the intended conciseness of this book, but Walter vehemently opposed me:

W: I do insist that we write down our discussions also on this topic, for two reasons: the first is that hardly any other term that should signal closeness to the Divine Power has been used with more devastating consequences than this father-son-syndrome!

B: I thought we would be economic with scientific expressions?

W: Sorry, but in order to describe this unholy order I had only this medical expression at hand, signifying disturbances in an organism who, taken together, create a definite pattern; I think that this also applies to the mind, not only to matter.

B: And the second reason?

W: We are putting down our discussions for men and women. Women, however, always got the short end in the Judaic-Christian tradition and consequently also in Islam. The term „Son" or „Son of Man" which is used indiscriminately for Yeshua the man and for the Logos speaking through him has contributed to and cemented the second-class status of women.

B: Where are we going to start?

W: I am beginning with our thesis that our planet is not a singular case within the cosmic revelation. Neither t h a t it happened here nor h o w it happened here. The Divine Power waives acts of mind-crushing self-revelations but uses representatives of the species to whom the revelation should go to, in every eligible habitat. Agreed so far?

B: We have no proof thereof, but it has a high degree of probability.

W: The biological evolution on our planet here offered only the alternatives of man or woman to be the medium. Why could it not have been a woman then?

B: You are sying that the Divine Power has had no alternative here?

W: Not in the sense of an irretrievable planning mistake, but paying tribute to a formation process of the human mind that had gone awry. This will become evident the moment you bother to start digging long before written history.

B: In the Stone Age?

W: Exactly. Now take over please and tell from our discussions where the roots of this misguided behaviour are, from which one half of this planet´s population is still suffering today!

B: Well, we have to go back 20.000 years indeed, if not more. If a family or tribe of hunters wanted to survive in these ages it had to be aggressive and mobile; if not, they became the victims of other tribes. We may safely assume that also a stone age woman and mother was prepared to fight, especially if her offspring were in danger. Mobility however was limited; the burden of pregnancy and the subsequent feeding and caring for the brood precluded her many times from participating in hunts or attacks on neighbouring tribes. Her role was not so much in battle but in logistics, we would say: dismembering the trophy, preservation of hides, keeping the fire alive, prepare food, care for supplies - and constantly her brood besides and over her and constant and unasked preparedness for copulation with the aim to produce sons, who could continue to fight and hunt.

W: Let me take over for a while. Only those who were able and called upon to kill were fully rated members of the tribe - which ruled out women. There already began the degradation of woman who was a useful, but not equal part of a man-dominated society. This did not change when hunters and gatherers gradually changed to animal husbandry or tilling the soil. The damage had been done already, the role of woman was preordained since these times: to serve, to please and to produce sons. Once written history sets in you may follow this assignment in countless variations and refinements, but it is engraved upon every culture. There are only a few and isolated instances in known history where matriarchy ruled. Nice enough we are finding a few pockets thereof still in Indonesia today.

B: The role of woman was written for her more than 20.000 years ago. Only now, in our age, they have found the will and voice to object. The degradation of woman was a derailment of the collective consciousness, governed largely by the inherited behaviour of species which we barely have begun to strip.

W: Are you not reducing everything here to bodily causes or charging it to the millions of years where the behaviour of species ruled and very successfully so?

B: Just wait a little, because now, with progressing history comes the infamy of the development. As collective consciousness increased the male part of the population may have recognized - or not - that there was an imbalance. But it was a very comfortable situation for man, so why change it? What was necessary now was a divine justification, later on an ethical one, much later a juridical one. Following that we must not be astonished that first the myths originated, fitting myths as e.g. on Eve, leading to ethics and laws by which the second-class status of woman was cemented. For man the world was in grandiose order; man-made laws received the supernatural label and were unassailable ever after.

W: Sometimes, when we pushed ourselves through the so-called Old Testament I shuddered how such a mode of thinking could be upheld. The priority in Abraham´s assets ranged from sons down to cattle, slaves, women and daughters.

B: All this was shame enough, but the worst was still to come. Under this scenario it was bound to happen also that the infertility or shortfalls of man´s mind meeded a practical excuse. What was more convincing than charging woman as the cause of missing male mental productivity? The temptatrix who, with her sensual appeals, hinders man to think or accomplish „great" things or to do the right, god-wanted. First of all, because as every animal, he is tired after copulation. Secondly, she ties man down to earth by ruining his high-flying thoughts by her demands for attention, taming of the children and for more household money. She is, therefore, not only a second-class human being, but also man´s spiritual burden. All centuries before us helped to paint this monstrous canvas, the ones brutal, others subtle, still others with a dab of humour - but all in the same manner.

W: I think we have explanations enough here to why Buddha was not happy with the idea of nuns´orders or why a Roman Pope decreed celibacy for the clergy in the 11th century. The „greatest christian philosopher of the Middle Ages" Thomas Aquinas, called woman - with a nod to his homophile Aristoteles - „something incomplete and irrelevant; probably she is the result of a passing debility in man´s force of copulation - or attributable maybe to the effects of a humid southern wind. A woman is a man who is lacking essential straits .... Man is the beginning and end of woman, just as God is the beginning and end of the cosmos", and so on in this vein ...

B: And they bought this pile of trash?

W: With gusto! He gave the supernatural blessings to the macho mind.

B: Didn´t he prepare also with this the moral ground for the witch-hunts of later centuries?

W: Yes, he and so many others.

B: I want to add one final argument: Islam is granting women certain rights, no doubt, which however end at the door-step mostly. The role of women in Islam is far more disgracing than in the so-called „christian" ones.

W: Agreed. So, let´s draw the line here. What happened? Again a reactor accident in the course of mental evolution?

B: I would not call it that. The evolution of the collective mind on this planet has come to the point where it sees the past development as a blind alley. In good evolutionary fashion the collective mind pulls out of the cul-de-sac and takes another course. We both agree that it is neither fast nor comprehensive enough and the biggest obstacles in the way are certainly the three big religions. Evolution, however, cannot be measured by decades.

W: I think we cleared the ground sufficiently. Now I am coming back to my contention that the Divine Power had no choice any more when she decided that our population was ripe for revelation. Always adhering to the thesis that she uses a representative of the population as her medium, this instrument could only be a man. A woman proclaiming that the Divine Power spoke from her would have survived only for hours.

B: The Hebrews would have stoned her to death immediately. The men of India, however, would have listened.

W: For a child is born to us, a daughter is given, and Her name shall be Marvelous, Wonderful, Counsellor and Princess of Peace. Do you notice in that twisted citation of Jesajah how inescapable this macho thinking had become already in this ethnic group?

B: We are not yet at the point. The Power speaking from Yeshua declared herself to be the Son of the God to whom the Hebrews prayed.

W: This gave two problems instead of one only: Yeshua the male and the Logos from within - both made the „Son"; and Yeshua neglected, according to all four reports on him, to keep this apart. Small wonder that this attitude steered the young church into her first and most dangerous dogmatic battle. He kept on saying that „I am the Son of God" - physique and all, when informing them that he existed before Abraham.

B: Could it have been a tribute to the state of mental evolution, especially of this ethnic group? The most intense relationship imaginable for them was the father-son tie. A mother-daughter relation in comparison to that rated next to nil in their set of values. Now, if the Spirit from within the male of Yeshua points to this relationship with the Divine Power, we almost could understand it, if we were conceited enough to say so. The male, the man were from this earth, however. We shall come back to this when we are discussing the theme of Resurrection in the second chapter.

W: Well, I see us fighting the Councils all over again. What for?

B: To show that the concept of a „Son" received a twist in the so-called christian churches that has barred the way to an evolutionary understanding of the teachings through Yeshua.

With „God from God, Light from Light, One Being with the „Father" - we can live with these rather nebulous phrases. But then human hyperbole struck: genitum, non factum! The obvious silly question after a female God could not take long to appear.

W: The Spirit from Yeshua speaks a clear language: it existed before this cosmos, in splendour not imaginable to man. All is given into its hand, and this „all" certainly is not only our planet or the galaxy we live in. The parable of the rebellious vineyard workers uses quite sharply the word „heir". And, so he states somewhere else, nobody can reach the „Father" but through him/her/it only. Our grammar has no gender for this phenomenon.

And, remember: there was nothing for which Yeshua was hated more by the priest caste than his claim to be the Son of God. Their God was not allowed to have a son, let be unimaginable multitudes of sons. Mohammed took over from here: there is only one God. And I do confess that I believe in that, too. There is only one Divine Power and we are barred to phantasize or know more about her manifestations, at least in this life.

B: Not so hasty, my friend. It is this Logos speaking through Yeshua that explicitly admits in some moments that there is no total identity between him/her/it and the „Father". Only „HE" knows the day and hour of the cataclysm in which our cosmos shall become a ball of fire. Not even he, the „Son", knows it. And this is not all, my friend: Yeshua says quite clearly that not „he" is speaking, clearly referring to his human physique, but how he hears, so he speaks and judges. In our words: the Divine Power „told" him what to say and when. He was not in possession of this power at all times, as may be seen in many instances, especially in the hours before his arrest. And lastly, also if it is anathema to many: the power in him did not like our population, our state of evolution. He/she/it clearly said that she - let us stay with this gender for short - did not come by her own will but was commanded to do so. So, again a fissure in the picture of „one being with the Father"! She sighed from within of Yeshua, for how much longer she had to stand this unintelligent species and to bear with its narrow margin of evolution.

W: What you want to say is that all this adds up to a „Minus X" in the power speaking from Yeshua, compared to the one God. Infinitesimal small, as it might be?

B: Yes. On the other hand there is an obvious contradiction in the reports: If all is given into the hands of the heir, it is all, without reservations, or it is not all.

W: I am just as unhappy over the notion of an „heir" as I am over the „son". In our state of mind the word „heir" immediately begets not only masculine but also dynastic dimensions: succession to the throne, transfer of power, resignation towards the follower; a God tired of administrating this cosmos - or more of them - retires. This reeks of human categories more than I can digest - anthropomorphism pure!

B: The tragedy of the whole issue is not our limited evolutionary horizon but the fact that discussions as we are having them now resulted in the physical destruction of tens of thousands in the past centuries, of those who could not imagine or believe a „father", „son", „heir", „trinity", „monophysique" of Yeshua but who believed in one God only whose being and manifestations are barred forever from our minds in this life.

W: The Baghavad-Gita in its 11th chapter could teach us the modesty that is required. There, in the most intense vocabulary of imagination is the admission of the impossibility to trace the manifestations of the Divine Spirit, „brighter than a thousand suns". It is a timeless acknowledgement of our limits, but also of the highest preparedness to venerate the Incomprehensible.

B: There is hardly more to say. Only a question to the end: do you think that our belief in the one Divine Power can tolerate contradictions, or better: „black boxes"?

W: I see this quite differently. W e , our embryonic evolutionary mind, are the black box. Hopefully the love of the Divine Power will tolerate that we are mixing up the issue quite often.

B: And now: no son?

W: No. And also no daughter, even if this possibility would have been evolutionary available.

B: What then?

W: The man and the male Yeshua. And the Spirit, the Logos, coming to us through him, which we have to take at his own value. And one Divine Power, forever.

B: I cannot refrain from remarking that in this Chapter we have confirmed Arius and his heresy quite successfully?

W: If he had available the evolutionary arguments at his days which we are having now, he would have been canonized. But his detractors still govern the so-called christian theology since roughly 1.700 years now.

B: Are we Arians?

W: No. We are evolutionary believers.

B: Neo-Arians?

W: The best thing now to do is to shut up. On things we are not able to talk about clearly we should not paste labels.

B: Didn´t we talk clearly?

W: We tried to as best as we could. We failed, however, because we cannot think or phantasize beyond our four-dimensional limits.

B: Perhaps we removed some ballast?

W: Not nearly enough, I suppose.

Atonement - What For ?

While Walter wanted to close the book on Jahve it was me who felt that still too much ballast was lying around, especially the one labeled „Atonement" and the other „Redemption". Walter argued that we scarcely could afford to throw our searchlight on many more requisites originating from the Hebrew conception which are blocking the evolutionary view to the revelation through Yeshua. But I argued back:

B: If it were that only, if we could close a chapter of cultural history which is self-explanatory, I would agree. The trouble is, however, that the notions I want to talk about have been embedded also in the credo of the so-called christian churches, with a devastating impact on the consciousness of those who wanted to believe the Spirit through Yeshua.

W: I agree that the chain of sin-atonement-redemption is rattling through the centuries, forged by Paul and willingly borne by Augustine and even Luther. But we wanted to write a concise book, didn´t we?

B: This we did. But last time you won the bargain and now its my turn. Then we are even, all right?

And I am starting right away into the subject:
The concept prevailing in the so-called christian churches is that of primeval guilt contracted by man against God, conveniently so and, because no attorney was around at this time, by Adam, substituting for the whole of mankind. May I remind you of the part attributed to Eve, substituting for the whole of womankind? The parable of the tree of life and the dessert of a harmless apple had to be believed literally still in our youth ...

W: I remember. Allegoric explanations were allowed only since Vaticanum II.

B: ... and now the consensus is that man/woman rebelled against the order of God and were punished consequently, so severely that they have not recovered from it until these days; this is why every newborn carries the stigma of not one but t h e primeval sin, a born rebel, that is. Of course this can be washed away only by baptism ...

W: ... yes, and for the infants that died without it they created the limbus puerorum, a murky sphere between heaven and hell, with a heavy spin towards non-existence.

B: That was an act of mercy - in their minds. But we are progressing too fast. When an Adam still had to be believed as a person it was not a very risky, but in fact a logical jump to the conclusion that atonement for his sin would - or should - be brought about by another personality, also by a man.

W: As by one man came death, and as in Adam everything died, everything was revived in Christ ...

B: You have read your Paul well. Here we are at the roots of this perverted thinking -

W: Aren´t you a little bit too harsh in your wording?

B: Not in the least. It was perverted in two ways. First, because Paul the Hebrew apparently did not care much about the rest population of the world. Remember that the Chinese culture was already 2.000 years old at his time, so were the Egyptians. But just as the Romans, they were the non-believers, a disgrace to God. Even though Paul was educated well they had no status with him. With Adam the w h o l e world was damned, period. Perversion no. 2: the individual never had a chance for atonement, for this was reserved by the scriptures for a Godsend who would atone for the sins „of the whole world", for the past as well as for the future ones. And only then the irate deity, one that could be insulted and f e l t much insulted, was reconciled again with the world.

W: I think you are not being fair to Paul. Probably he had no idea of the existence of the Chinese culture, even if probability speaks against it. His „world" was Judaism plus Jahve.

B: That is just the pity of it, and very convenient. But when he started his mission travels he must have met people who told him that there are cultures also East of Athens? There is no mentioning of them.

W: He must have had a singular track of mind, that of a fanatic.

B: In fact he is giving me the shivers, and not only in the issue we are discussing just now. The so-called Christian churches were of a different opinion; they accorded him ex post the assistance of the Divine Spirit, something they are upholding even these days.

W: Very strange indeed. I still hear the curse echoing that he hurled in one of his letters to the non-believers in Christ. Divine Spirit? On the other hand, if they would retract on this now, their whole precarious edifice of faith would tumble - much faster.

B: The detergent for sins, in Paul´s notion, is blood, human blood. Not anybody´s blood or that of ritually slaughtered animals, but the blood of the „Son of God", Yeshua´s. Only because blood streamed from Yeshua´s tortured body, reaching the ground, this world and we are saved.

W: I think that the respective lines in his letters are simply repulsive. If no other means of pacifying the insulted deity was acceptable than the blood and the physical crushing of a Messiah then this deity ranges in good style with Moloch, but not with the Logos talking through Yeshua.

B: The power to forgive sins was not left to the contrite person itself however much he/she felt sorry, but to Yeshua´s followers who ended in a priest caste, certainly not wanted by the Logos. Luther was daring enough to do away with this notion; confession, however, is still the rule with the rest of the so-called Christian churches.

W: Let us depart from this sad story and look at something else. The concept of sin originated in the Hebrew faith as a misbehaviour against the rules of Jahve. If it had been the Ten Commandments only then life would have be relatively easy because the wordly criteria therein were covered by secular law also in other societies- Hammurabi again - as an accepted code of ethics; they needed no supernatural origin. It was their barricade of ritual laws, however, which made things becoming more and more unbearable because even the most orthodox believer would stumble over one of the 613 rules at least once a day.

B: The four reports on Yeshua give us a good account of the perverted - sorry, again - way of thinking that had developed. Form over content, ritual over nature, law over spirit. The saddest lines in the four reports are those where the Logos through Yeshua tries to find a chink in their arrogant armour and, very soon, sees that the evolution of consciousness had reached another dead end here. Therefore he gives up to argue with them and just exposes their intransigence to public ridicule. And that was Yeshua´s death verdict.

W: Of course, we have become a little complacent with the increase of knowledge in the natural sciences and, above all, in the science of behaviour. With the older parts of our brain, which made us survive as primates, we joyfully murdered, angered, robbed, fornicated and multiplied. Trouble is, we would like to be rid of them now, but there is no way. The inherited behaviour of species cannot be operated or washed away but is still very much in control. I doubt very much again that this development should have been enacted, or will be, in other habitats where reflexive thinking will have/has had a breakthrough; I hope that evolution there will be able at least to skip cannibalism.

What I want to say is, in short: if we are running around with this mortgage we are entitled to a bonus of forgiveness, isn´t it?

B: I put it differently: increasing social behaviour has already erected dams that are high and sturdy enough to ward of the nagging waves of primeval behaviour in our brains. Until our cranium will take over fully in the way that we eliminate these strains as abnormal, a considerable evolutionary period will be necessary.

The Logos has planted the flag already at the other end of the course. Through Yeshua we know precisely, in our cranium, what the expectations in us are - even in the present transformation stage.

W: And if we revolt to these expectations or stumble over a number of them day by day - is this sin which needs atonement?

B: I think you have mixed up the issue. If we are revolting against them we are saying that they are too high at any rate, but besides also unnatural, impractical, cruel - and evil! With that, I think, we have forfeited the love offered to us, have committed the „sin against the spirit" which is apparently unforgiveable. The day-by-day stumbling is quite different. The main thing is to stand up again after every slip.

W: And to say „Sorry"!

B: Simply: forgive me! In whatever form or language you say it.

W: And you are sure that you are forgiven after that?

B: Yes, and so are you, I know. And we are taking much comfort in that, isn´t it?

Resurrection - In What ?

B: Before we have not dealt with the concept of resurrection here we have not cleared the path for an evolutionary understanding in the next chapter, which we called „Space Probes", don´t you think?

W: So you think we should get rid of some more ballast?

B: Indeed I do. It is one of the most voluminous and most superfluous packages that have been saddled on an evolutionary understanding of the message coming through Yeshua.

W: Couldn´t we simply kick it from our sleigh and be done with it?

B: I am afraid not. Too much is connected to it, both ways: in the traditional Jewish/ Christian and Moslem belief and much more to the mainstream concept of a universal evolution which we will discuss in the next chapter.

W: I agree. We have not only to be honest this time, but hurting, almost surgical without anestethics, do you realize that?

B: May the Divine Power help us.

W: Like any good analysts we have to define the terms of our discussion first. What is resurrection?

B: I am pushing ten thousand pages of venerable writing plus fifty councils aside, with all due respect, and say in my evolutionary belief: after bodily death, the personality of the being will go on to exist in a state of being and in dimensions of which we cannot have the slightest notion or fantasy. This personality needs not its former three-dimensional format any more.

W: I shall carry on, if you please: in contrast to India´s venerable ideas, this personality is not an infinitesimal part of the so-called „Great Being", having existed before in innumerable reincarnations until the one we are burying now. No.
Genes of a terrestrial father and mother have produced me. I am a three-dimensional product, and yet there is more to me. But how much more?

B: This „more", in our opinion, is the personality. Our terrestrial science, especially the behavioral ones, accord us the patterns of behaviour of the primates of our planet, which we still carry in the old brain formations.
The „personality", however, is the revolutionary side, to say so, to this pattern of stone age behaviour.
The more „revolutionary" we become to eradicate these ingrained structures, the more „evolutionary" we become in the understanding of the Divine Power which used Yeshua as its mouthpiece.

W: Understood. But how far up, or down, reaches this „personality"?

B: You mean, if we put our miserable human condition as the calibrating gauge to this?

W: You have struck me down before I could declare war.

B: When I said „miserable human condition" I felt not miserable at all. Because from the height we have reached in consciousness we are able to accord us a cognitive processing of information, reflexive thinking. Looking down the ladder of evolution, i.e. in animal and plant life, there is no reflexive thinking. Our scientists make an artificial distinction of „phenomenal awareness" which in our language means that e.g. the butterfly is „somehow aware" that it must get closest to a light source even if this may be its end.
Then there is the „learning capacity", which fish and bees already have. And close up to us on the ladder rungs comes the blissful love of our dogs and horses who certainly have their way of saying „I love you", and we understand them silently and fully.
To come back to our starting point: we are very well able to look down the ladder and to stick arbitrary grade labels of consciousness on plants and animals. But looking up the ladder we see only fog. Some people really believe that we are standing at the end of the ladder, which is, in evolutionary concepts, simply megalomania, delusion of grandeur.

W: This is all very interesting but could you please come back to the salient point of our discussion: what is going to be resurrected?

B: One thing is quite certain: it will not be the „flesh", if we take this word as a synonym for any tangible carrier of consciousness, e.g. here, on this planet, our three-dimensional body.

W: And why not, please? Don´t you like your body or what?

B: I would have expected a more refined question. But talking back in your vernacular, I am asking you simply if Stephen Hawking likes his body?

W: Touché. I apologize.

B: Accepted. I want to bulldoze aside a notion which we have inherited or which is staring down on us from thousands of church paintings, but which still commands the dogmatic idiocy of a bodily resurrection i.e. the bodily assumption of Mirijam into the Unknown. Apart from the a-sexual notions on Mirijam´s body it is apparently the body, even if transfigured in Paul´s notion, that is needed in the ultimate dimension as a sort of passport. The bearer must still be recognizable, as he/she was in his/her mortal packaging.

W: A wise Persian philosopher shuddered at the idea of having to look at the same old faces again after resurrection.

B: So would I.

W: Not to speak of the physical appearances of peoples of other habitats?

B: Is´nt it funny? All directors of science-fiction films try to surpass each other in the ugliness and depravity of alien beings, murderous mostly. So far no film was made, but will come hopefully, that depicts the story from the other side: that intelligent beings of a highly advanced grade of intellect really swoop down on us, but not to exterminate us, no. For them we look bizarre, to say the least, if not downright repulsive. Curious extremities. Underdeveloped cranium. Reproduce like the animals they are killing and eating. Gravity has allowed them a certain body height and mass. They show a hostile behaviour. Why?
What I want to underline is that nobody, not from this planet nor from any other in this galaxy nor from any other in millions of them will ever need its refined replica in the ultimate dimension after bodily death, simply because they would continue to shudder or laugh at each other for a whole eternity.

W: If not, how will the Divine Power keep the spirits of them apart? How will it judge them if they are not clear-cut personalities? And: how will you recognize your parents again, wife, children?

B: I do not know. But I believe that they also will be really existing personalities in the same way I shall be. The mechanism of how we meet again, do we want to meet again certain personalities at all, or how we communicate - all this we shall not know in this life.

W: The Logos in Yeshua gave the Sadduceans a clear concept of the life thereafter. The main message of his answer was: the body plays no role in the ultimate dimension.

B: Now we are galloping into the home run, my friend. I also believe in his explanation of the being in the ultimate dimension, as he struck down the unsavory sexual notion of their parable. But by doing so he also became the anti-interpretation of a God to be eaten as bread or drunk as wine or to have resurrected bodily from a rock grave: matter plays no role in the ultimate state of being.

W: Careful, my friend! If you deny the bodily resurrection of Yeshua, you are digging at the very foundations of Christian belief!

B: And how I dig! If their belief, as Paul has recklessly enough taught them, is depending on this pivotal criterium, that of the bodily resurrection of Yeshua called the Christ, then he led them into the desert because the body, also that of a Yeshua, returns his ingredients to this earth. Full Stop. In other habitats this will apply also, in whatever molecules.

W: Let us come to the ultimate denial then: The man Yeshua, called the Christ, did not resurrect in his terrestrial body?

B: Certainly not, and there was no supra-natural necessity to do so.

W: But the so-called „Christian" churches are basing their total faith system on fact that he did. And, they say, because he did so as the first since Adam, we are able to resurrect now also - in a transfigured body as Paul hastened to add.

B: Again, and without condescension, we are looking at people that believe in a God that is too small. The Divine Power simply smiles at them and the evolution goes up another rung on the ladder.

W: Please do not get carried away! Where is the corpse of Yeshua?

B: I trust and hope that it has been buried, not mummified.

W: The angel figures in the reports tell a different story. They simply stated „that he is not here any more", which is not very informative.

B: He, Yeshua, was very much „here", if this means our planet. His „existence" was, following the reports, erratic, changeable, tangible if so wanted for non-believers, going through matter like walls and doors, obfuscating the eyes of those who were near to him for more than two years i.e., binding the eyes e.g. of two believers in the village of Emmaus - is this bodily resurrection, even as a transfigured terrestrial body as Paul wanted to have him?

W: Again: where is the body of Yeshua?

B: I do not know. And what is more: it is not important!

W: And what about the resurrection of our body?

B: I am glad that my body will not resurrect. I could not stand myself - and that is hardly a question of age.

W: Are you positive that we shall recognize each other in the ultimate dimension?

B: Not only that, my friend. Much more important is that the Divine Power will keep all those aligned who have corresponded to her universal demand of tolerance, pity and love.

W: Are we reborn?

B: Yes. And in a fashion that shames Paul for all times.

W: We are not through yet. I have no difficulty to believe that the personality - for me a synonym with „soul" - should live on in a spiritual world. But what about the personalities of animals whom we love, especially those who are returning this love, personally and specifically? How is their „personality" rated by the Divine Power, in order to accord them also a spiritual existence?

B: Everybody here knows that you and your Irish setter Anshi are inseparable. And yet you doubt that the Divine Power knows the love between you two also? Do you really believe that this love would simply be extinguished, like a candle is blown out? Never. I am sure that this love will be transformed gloriously also, especially this kind of unquestioning love that we receive from responsive animals only.

W: You are a great comfort, thank you. But my personal feelings aside: would it apply to any animal or do we have to draw the line somewhere on the „personality"? Or asked in another way: how much personality has a three-month-old human baby that dies?

B: I am not drawing a line between the baby and, say, a pony. For once, both of them receive love and register this very well. And, according to the responsive mechanisms that evolution has given them, they return this affection, clearly directed back, loving individuals. For me, this love is, and will be, preserved forever.

W: And what about animals with a lesser amount of „personality"? Take a fish, frog, rabbitt?

B: We must not make the mistake to judge the possibility of their „resurrection" on the grade of how one of them was loved, or not loved, by a human being. This is irrelevant. I am of the debatable opinion that any grading of personality should be tied to an individual´s potential to give love. If so, then this love is certainly transferable into the ultimate dimension, together with its objects. This I believe quite fervently.

W: The pair of swans that stays together for life?

B: Where is the difference between them and a pair of humans? Marginal only.

W: Do you look forward with joy to your resurrection?

B: I hope that my joy will atleast balance my fear.

W: Shall we meet again in the next life?

B: Look for me, will you?

Poor, Great Mirjam

Walter and I grew up in the Catholic part of Bavaria where the veneration of Mirijam has an unshakeable place in the minds of the true believers. It is veneration, still, and not worshipping of a female deity as it is felt, knowingly or not, in the East and Southern European or Latin American countries. The degree of veneration that should be accorded to her has become again a matter of hot debate these days since a Polish pope is clearly not able to step down on those who want a higher rank for her than just being the terrestrial mother of Yeshua.

So there is ballast galore, as on so many other concepts that stand in the way of an evolutionary understanding of the revelation through her also terrestrial, short-lived son.

Walter and I debated for a long time whether we should dedicate the last section of this chapter to this great woman. In the end we felt that it was necessary, especially in the face of the „Mary-For-Goddess" movement which is spreading like wildfire these days. Please listen to our discussion:

B: How could it happen that this doubtlessly great woman should reach a form of veneration in the biggest so-called christian church, that is sometimes tantamount to adoration?

W: I see a number of reasons, beginning with the first:
The revenge God of the so-called Old Testament became in the Hebrew belief the God of love and mercy very late only and so his image was transported into the so-called christian beliefs - but not for long.

Of course he was presented as God-Father, but much more to be afraid of than to be truly loved, especially by women.

In a church which is largely impervious to terrestrial terror, squalor, health and life of its unasking followers it is only natural that women, mothers especially, turned to somebody to whom they could reach out in their despair, to somebody closest to Yeshua, to Mirijam.

B: So you think that this exaggerated degree of veneration is less due to her personality, of which we know very little indeed, but much more so to the glacial distance of a „Father" and an escape from the unbending consequences of a „Son"?

W: Yes. In contrast to all the havoc which the so-called christian beliefs and sects wrought with the revelation through Yeshua Mirijam stood for all which distinguishes a mother since milleniums: patience, understanding, holding fast, forgiving, hoping - and loving.

B: I share your view. Small wonder therefore that within an unforgiving belief Mirijam became the port of pleas for all those whose terrestrial needs received scant attention by official churches, on the contrary, which compounded their misery. But where are the other reasons?

W: In the fact that Yeshua once was a baby and child for whom a good mother cared. Every mother afterward could expect and hope that her worries would be listened to much more and easier by a mother Mirijam than by an impersonal and remote deity.

B: I am going even further: Mirijam became a spiritual asylum into which also those could flee who suffered murder and torture from the hands of the priest churches or from the secular powers which were obedient to them. Mirijam´s many-painted, many-cited mantle of protection for which men and women prayed alike was not only conceived as a shield against pestilence, hunger and war, but also against the murderers in the frocks of monks, prelates, bishops and popes - down to the last witch burning 1738 in Glarus, Switzerland.

W: I see one more reason which reaches back very far into cultural history and is, possibly one of the most salient therefore. Already 5.000 years ago people, not only women, found it easier to pray to a mother deity, whether she was called Ishtar, Kybele, Isis or Demeter. At any rate far easier than to adore the deity Moloch, to whom they had to sacrifice their children, or a sex-crazy Jove.

B: So it is. Also the Jahve of Israel certainly was not a very inviting deity for a woman in sorrow.

W: Let us get back to the roots of our information. One of the four reporters, who never met Yeshua, gives us a heart-warming story of the a-sexual conception and birth of Yeshua ...

B: Yes, it is difficult not to feel the gilded charm of this legend.

W: And what about the truth, essence of the story?

B: For that we should leaf back a few pages in cultural history. There we see the parallels where the conception and birth of most of the great religious minds has been adorned at later times with a supranatural explanation. The narration of the supranatural conception of the prince Gautama, later Buddha, is in no way less beautiful than the rosegarden of Luke.

W: Thank you for leading me to my next point, which has apparently been cast aside as unimportant by all narrators: looking at it closely it was only a half-human or half-godly conception, i.e. without a terrestrial father, but with a very real terrestrial mother with all her organism. So: a supranatural DNA string unites with the terrestrial DNA string of the mother and - voilá - the product is supranatural?

B: This, I think, should finish with the notion that the baby, boy, man Yeshua is of supranatural origin or that he was destined to serve as the speaker of the Divine Power „ab ovo", literally, since his mother´s egg was fertilized.

W: As a side thought, since when in his life, do you think, was his mission clear to him?

B: The reports on him give a quite uniform account on that: when he insisted to be baptized in the Jordan by Yochanaan.

W: But it is reported that this Yochanaan recognized him immediately as the Chosen one, before baptizing him?

B: We have the explanation also in the reports. One one occasion Yeshua stated that in Yochanaan was the returned spirit of Eliah, unfathomable for us in this life.

W: Let´s go back to our immediate concern. How did Yeshua see his mother? The four reports certainly do not paint a very deep or respectful relationship going out from him, quite on the contrary!

B: He is never calling her „mother", but only „woman" and that in a sometimes chilly fashion -

W: I think that she suffered very much by his treatment, because she loved him as her first-born, probably much more than his brothers and sisters.

B: Is it possible that Mirijam had other children after him?

W: The so-called christian churches don't like this idea at all, but it has been clearly and unmistakably so reported. Four brothers are mentioned by name, the sisters are referred to simply as such - they did not count in a male society.

B: I think we have to discuss her husband Yussuf also, don't you think so?

W: Certainly I do, but first the basic question again: why was Yeshua so cold and abrasive to his bodily mother?

B: I do not think that your choice of words is helpful. When the Logos spoke from Yeshua, then these words were not those of Yeshua the man. The Spirit in him saw the terrestrial mother of Yeshua very well, but he put her under a higher rating, genderless, that of a human being which responds to his call.

W: So was she called upon, as is reported, by the angel Gabriel?

B: There or later, it is not important for the message coming through Yeshua. To put it sharply and candidly: it is absolutely not important whether Mirijam stayed a virgo intacta. And: the concept of a supranatural spiritual implantation of one half of Yeshua's genes into a virginal womb may be believed or not - it is of no consequence for the appearance and call of the Logos through Yeshua .

W: For me she has gained greatness already by the fact that she did not waver but stood it through to observe the slow dying of her son on the cross.

B: It seems to me that out of the whole range of followers she was the only one who believed unflinchingly in his mission. And she knew that her child was dying up there, not a God.

W: Yes, she was a singularly strong woman. But is this enough to see her today as a mediatrix between us and the Divine Power and to accord her almost divine status?

B: Of course this is a wild exaggeration of her role and personality. And what is more: we need no mediator nor mediatrix to address the Divine Power. Luther made this clear once and for all.

W: But people turn to her for help, the world over?

B: It is the same with the countless saints to whom the believers of the so-called christian churches turn for assistance. For one, they are afraid to address the Divine Power directly, because they have no concept of her being nor of her all encompassing, evolutionary love. For the other, it is much more simple to have a lawyer who is looking after your interests and who will plead with the judge.

I do not want to mock myself at the worries and utter despair of those who try this way - but they simply have not enough trust in the Creator. And the same holds true for the cries of help to Mirijam which are floating up to her around the globe without interruption. Despairing of the church organizations which are run by men, they also despair of a „Father" and of a „Son". The mother is the last resort, as any child knows.

W: I want to ask you precisely: is it legitimate that we address ourselves to Mirijam for help?

B: „Legitimate" - that does not meet the point. Of course it is legitimate. But it is hardly evolutionary, if we believe in the existence of countless other habitats in the universe where intelligent beings exist - hopefully not suffering as our world population. For them there has never been the like of Mirijam and will never be. But the Divine Power has been, and will be.

W: Should we talk about Yussuf, her husband, now?

B: Oh yes! Yeshua was known in the reports as the son of Yussuf, the carpenter. We may safely assume that Yeshua, being the son and heir, learnt this profession from his father.

W: The churches have not done Yussuf justice. In all artistic imaginations he looks more like Yeshua´s grandfather.

B: Of course. The churches wanted to signal that after Yeshua there were nor more offsprings from this couple and - consequently - Yussuf led a celibate life besides Mirijam ever after.

W: What a nonsense! Yussuf I can imagine as a young, healthy, good-looking man and Mirijam, his wife, also as a healthy and probably beautiful woman. And - their other children are on record. We may safely assume, therefore, that Mirijam and Yussuf lived for years happily in the Hebrew marital tradition. What else?

B: But someday there must have been a fight between Yeshua and his father. A basic fight, on Yeshua´s future. Someday Yeshua found out that his vocation was not with carpentry but with the word of God - and he left. His father remained probably in a state of fury, because the heir threw before his feet the shattered hopes of carrying on the enterprise, of having a nice daughter-in-law and grandchildren - whatever.

W: It is remarkable that, apart from the Lost & Found story at their Jerusalem journey Yussuf is not emerging any more in the reports. It is only a fair assumption on my side that the marriage of Yussuf and Mirijam later went sour over Yeshua - or that Yussuf died before Yeshua went public. We only hear from her in the reports.

B: I have heard much wilder theories than yours about Yussuf, but they are purely fictional. In my opinion he was a brave and solid man.

W: And Mirijam?

B: She was the first believer and had an immense capacity for love, patience and enduring. She was truly a great woman.

W: But not somebody to whom we owe tribute or an exclusive access to God, or, as the Polish pope would like to see her, as Co-Redemptrix?

B: Nothing divine, simply one of the greatest women this earth has carried, for sure.

Chapter II:

SPACE PROBES

Whether Or Not To Write This Chapter

When Walter and I drafted the table of contents for our small book this chapter was the most controversial issue in the whole project. We are not going to bother you for pages with arguments and counter-arguments; the short version went like this:

B: In the first chapter we pushed some ballast from the sleigh. Since we are still on an expedition, how are we going to call our next chapter?

W: Depends on what we plan to do. We are trying to start a few weather balloons by which we hope to get some insights on the climate above our heads which is closed forever to our three- or four-dimensional deduction, induction, fantasy. Wait! We cannot reasonably expect glimpses of an order that is unfolding throughout the universe.

What we can expect, however, are matching questions to answers which are given to us in the revelation through Yeshua since 2000 years already - especially the evolutionary answers which have not been dared to be seen that way.

B: How could they? The concept of evolution is hardly 150 years old. Do you believe in earnest that we, like gold diggers, shall retrieve some unnoticed nuggets of truth out of the four reports? This is preposterous! Everything has been already thought once; this has been said by a prominent Islamic philosopher, and very justly so!

W: If we were of this opinion we could have scrapped the project of our book from the very beginning. No. No! No! Why are we having these discussions and write them down? Because we are of the opinion that n o t everything has been thought, n o t everything has been asked, especially n o t within an evolutionary concept of the message through Yeshua!

B: Please calm yourself! What you want to say is that this Yeshua has already given answers to questions which only our generation, with its increased evolutionary consciousness is able to raise?

W: Exactly this way I see it! Be it questions seeking matching answers in the revelation through Yeshua, be it probabilities which are still covered by an evolutionary interpretation - we are after them both!

B: Then this is more than weather balloons. These will be space probes!

W: Thank you, my friend! This will be the heading of our second chapter, naturally! They are not meant to bring back quantitative data as manned space flights, this is ridiculous; but what they can bring back are justified probabilities on the power field of the revelation coming through Yeshua, a power field that is detectable only to the evolutionary inquiry of the human mind.

B: Stay on the carpet. Do you realize that hundreds of millions of men and women have pored over the revelation through Yeshua; that thousands felt compelled to communicate their impressions or „revelations" to the world; that among these thousands, hundreds did so at acute peril of life - and now you are coming and saying that in this monumental canvas there might still be white spots which we, w e !, are going to fill in! Are you still on the carpet?

W: Very much so. You may call me arrogant a thousand times, only go on with the expedition, don´t give up here! The canvas comparison, which you gave, is a very good one. But not white spots, they would have been detected very early.

It is the p e r s p e c t i v e which has deceived the viewers over the centuries. Relatively unimportant elements command the stage; the truly important ones, those which point far above our habitat, have been shoved to the sidelines - not by ill will, no - only because their momentum was not grasped, could not be grasped with a human intelligence that was devoid of natural science, social behaviour and evolutionary concept. Our generation is endowed with all these. This is our justification to put new questions to the message coming through Yeshua in this chapter. I have no idea as yet about the outcome. Are you coming aboard now?

B: Step aside!

Evolution, The Kingway Of Creation

W: If we want to be understood in the next sections we have to put an explanation at the beginning of this chapter, otherwise the following thoughts have no basis. Right?

B: On target. Evolution, this grandiose view that the natural sciences have opened to us since Darwin can be understood by us only along the backward pointing arrow of time, so we are told, but we can have no knowledge, or imagination, where this process of creating ever more complex and ever more beautiful forms of life will lead us to.

W: One insight, however, has reached the grade of common belief in all human minds: that our human species has been privileged so far by the evolution on this planet, no doubt, but that we are far from any point of culmination; and secondly, that by the sheer time span that was needed to develop us from the protoplasma cell it is safe to assume that there are habitats in the universe who have had an earlier start to develop intelligent life. Having had it, they have advanced far more compared to us and we shall never make good the distance.

On the other hand, we are far advanced compared to other habitats where the process has set in a billion years ago, or fifty millions years ago, or yesterday. On a universal scale, our species is not privileged at all.

B: You are aware that we are walking a high rope without a net. The most welcome net would be the first proven existence of planets outside of our solar system, a very comforting net indeed.

W: As we follow the scientific reports this has happened last year only (1997). I think we may safely consider this to be one of our strongest nets. But I want to add something very important. Be it on a cosmic scale or down here on our speck of dust, the scientists point out that evolution, in their sense, has no fixed direction, is not following a given master plan, that it operates by trial and error, „learns" fast, does this and that. The more you listen to them the more you gain the impression that, on one hand, they accord her an acting and decision capacity, on the other they think of evolution only in terms of the sum of all mutations that originated by chance during five billion years.

B: And this is why you and me have said a respectful „No" to the view of the natural scientists. For us, evolution certainly has a direction, if we believe in the revelation of the Divine Power through Yeshua. Woven into a universal pattern it is the evolution of ever more complex matter first that gives substance to the development of life.

This level is followed by the evolution of intelligent life and beings that have the power of reflexive thinking. This is our present stage, for instance. We still need a body to transport our consciousness. Because we cannot look into the future we have not the least imagination what the next plateau of evolution could look like for our human race. But two things are certain already now: for one, that plateaus of ever higher consciousness are „in store" for our species, if she will be physically existant for a couple of millions of years from now; secondly, and there we are coming back to Yeshua: there is already consciousness in this universe that needs no vehicle of physical matter but is self-contained in a way which is not understandable nor dreemable in our life span here.

W: Suppose you are right and evolution i s   acting purposefully, to what purpose then, please?

B: Here we come to the crucial point. In my belief, it is the creation of beings with reflexive thinking and a free will and, lastly, to unite these beings in spiritual form with their Creator, the Divine Power that spoke through Yeshua - if they accept this offer.

W: In their own free will?

B: The message through Yeshua was this offer, to the free will of our species. It can be accepted or be thrown out in corporate form or by any individual and on any planet.

W: What you say is very moving, but it lacks any proof, even probability.

B: Proof, yes. Probability - no. One of the tenets of natural science still is that the universe surrounding us is, in the broadest scale, materially more or less the same in every corner of the observable cosmos; take the distribution of matter, for instance, or the validity of the law of physics -

W: - the latter has been seriously questioned already -

B: Never mind. The material universe is of the same basic structure anywhere. The Creator, in whom we both believe, put more than hydrogen, time, and the laws of nature into the crib of the universe. He also added evolution, but not as a fourth component; it was embedded already in all three others.

W: Do you want to say that evolution was, and still is, the creative will of the Divine Power?

B: Thank you for this word. Yes, exactly so. The parallel and sound probability which we may draw from the findings of natural science is the following, therefore: In a universe that holds a uniform distribution of matter there is also a uniform will by its Creator if you believe in one, and we do. „Evolution" is the concept that comes closest to the „intention" of the Creative, Divine Power that we heard out of Yeshua.

W: What happens to evolution in a habitat that has said „No, thank you!" to the offer of the Divine Power? Will it be switched off there?

B: Your choice of words is too flippant now. No, of course not. Also these habitats will march on from one plateau to the next of consciousness, they will quite „naturally" shed their bodily vehicles at later stages, and - this we hear through Yeshua - they have united their forces already.

W: Star wars?

B: Not beautiful fairy tales for grown-ups. Stark, immensely powerful - the opposite universal will. But we are reserving a section of this chapter for this phenomenon.

W: Hard to believe. That way you are declaring evolution to be blind, do you realize that? If it continues to „work" also in habitats that have thrown out the offer of the Divine Power, together with the do´s and don´ts she is putting forward, this is tantamount to high treason to the habitats that have united their will with the Creator, or?

B: If the Divine Power would not recognize and, yes, respect free will of created beings this universe would be just one big puppet theatre with the Great Puppeteer dangling us from his strings.

W: Granted. But what happens ultimately with the dissenters?

B: This is one of the space probes that we are going to launch in this chapter.

The Perpetual Revelation

B: It is again the natural sciences that have blasted clear the trail of understanding that our planet is not an evolutionary singularity in the cosmos. We know very well how stars are born. If you look at the pictures the Hubble Space Observatory is bringing down, you get very small and very proud at the same time: millions of galaxies with trillions of suns - it is breathtaking and yet very comforting.

W: Comforting in what way?

B: Because we see that we are not a preferred or singular habitat in the universe. And if we accept that from the scientific point of view - and we do - then it is safe to assume that also our human species is in no way preferred before a Creator. We are certainly unique in our temporal physical appearance. But evolution and gravity are shaping forms of life in the universe that are unimaginable to us.

W: I have already difficulty enough if I look back on our ancestry on this planet, and living as a contemporary to a butterfly, an orchid or an elephant.

B: So it is. But coming back to the universal scale: also our level of consciousness, our ability to analyze our thinking, is not a preferred phase which evolution has reserved for our species only.

W: Of course not. Why are you stressing this fact?

B: Because it is obvious so far only from the scientific approach. What has been not been anchored in the mind of man, however, is the deduction which becomes justified on this basis: that any species in the universe, on any habitat, which grows into this evolutionary stage, will receive the revelation by the Divine Power - and only then, because she cannot reveal herself to an amoeba.

W: Are you inferring that there is a „must" for the Divine Power?

B: In a way, yes. Since we believe in the love to her creatures, which pervades all four reports on Yeshua, we cannot see her as the detached chief engineer of evolution who is dismissing unsuccessful tests with a shrug and starts the next series.

(B): Do not ask me what makes our species, for instance, loveable! I find many reasons why it is detestable, something which also the Logos from Yeshua said occasionally. But the revelation is clear in this respect: we are loved by our Creator.

Since we are not alone nor unique in the cosmos, it follows that also all other habitats are encompassed in this love. If this is the case, then the Divine Power „must" reveal herself at some point in the history of a habitat - at the point where reflexive thinking has set in there.

W: Are you having any indication from the reports on Yeshua that this is so, or could be so?

B: Yes, we have: there are many mansions in the house of my Father. And: I have also sheep not from this stable to whom I have to tend to.

W: In this context these sentences begin to shine in a different light.

B: Yes, in the universal sense in which they were intended all along.

W: This invariably brings us around to the „task" of revelation.

If we assume the number of habitats in our galaxy coming to the point of reflexive consciousness as, say, 10^6 as a conservative estimate, then you have the same number of necessary revelation processes, the same number of „sons" of God i.e. the same number of „Yeshua´s" - this is mind-boggling!

B: The same number of „Yeshua´s" - yes. Because we believe that the revelation is channelled through a member of the species to which it is going - as here on this earth. But not a corresponding number of „sons" of God - because there is only the one Logos that spoke also through our Yeshua - and will communicate through chosen representatives in each and every habitat that rises to the power of understanding.

W: In my words - if this process can ever be expressed in words - you are seeing the revelation not as a sequence but as a continuum?

B: Would you care to explain that?

W: In a sequence one thing happens after the other in time. In a continuum things happen parallel to each other at the same time, phased, and constantly.

B: Looking at it this way the revelation certainly is a continuum. It is a little bit awkward to talk about the notion of time, or even of a concept of „at the same time" in the universe, since Einstein and Hawking. But if we say that the revelation must not „come" to a habitat in the sense a radio signal travels to it, but „has been there" already since the beginning of time, encompassing it as the space and time around it, and that the growing consciousness of a habitat rises like a reflector to it - then we probably are at the beginning of understanding and also at the end of our vocabulary.

W: I want to put a very clear question to you: do you believe that during the life of Yeshua there were „at the same time" other processes of revelation going on in the universe?

B: Millions of them, I am sure. And I felt the quotation marks in your voice, thank you.

W: Will most of them also kill their „Yeshua´s"?

B: Most of them - hardly. Some of them - yes. In whatever way „killing" may be effected there - but the contemporaries silenced them. If they were able to laugh, perhaps they silenced the bearer this way.

At any rate, some did not accept the revelation, the fact that God is and God cares. They had no necessity for it.

W: Do you notice how we are using the past tense only? Is it conceivable that at this very moment where we are discussing, revelations are occurring above our heads, and will occur - millions and millions of them?

B: No. It is not conceivable, but believable, and we find great comfort in it. And it takes away the last rest of a hubris that we, or our earth, should be privileged by the Divine Spirit in any way.

How Evil Is Evil ?

W: Any criticism of the revelation of the Divine Power through Yeshua invariably comes up with the argument that this God cannot be omnipotent since he is not able to eradicate the Evil from his creation. Their argument is bolstered by the parable of the field with good seed - God´s creation of the universe - on which his wily opponent sowed weeds during the night. Immediately the reasoning begins: Was this God aware of the fact that he had an opponent? If not so, he is not omniscient. If he was aware, however, why did he not stop him?

Either he was not able to do so, that is, weak, or he decided not to intervene for the sinister reason that from now on there would be temptation among his creatures on which they could test their free will.

The end of the prayer which Yeshua taught his followers seems to underline this notion. For if we have to beg our Creator not to lead us into temptation this cannot mean anything else than that this Power is setting up traps for our conscience, tempering the iron, pruning the vine, - and what if the creature fails the test?

B: Let me finish it for you: the creature will be thrown out into darkness, not to perish there, no, but to suffer there forever. Right?

W: You are trying to mock me. But these are the very words of the Logos speaking from Yeshua, of a loving God, a caring Father, of a Holy Spirit that is synonym to universal love -

B: - and instead of love and forgiveness you are reaping fire, brimstone and torture - forever.

W: If you do not believe me, then pick up the four reports and read for yourself again. Apparently you have forgotten these parts or tried to suppress them from your thinking?

B: Not for a minute. I share your view that this part of the revelation seems to have a self-destructive element in it, and predestination was the almost logical outcome for warped and feeble human minds.

W: We were hardly able to suck in a breath of relief when the Logos from Yeshua began to reveal a Divine Power that has compassion and understanding, in contrast to the deity of the so-called Old Testament - and then this blood-thirsty Yahve arises formidably in the background again - awaiting us with an eternal order in which there are only sheeps and muttons. Poor muttons; how did they ever think that they could attain the status of sheep?

B: There is no need for this dejected attitude, my friend. What we have to do is to have a structured discussion of this whole complex, a very courageous discussion, and not to stare agonized at the grand painting in the Capella Sistina or to listen to Dante dishing out all the sadistic details of hell.

When we started this chapter we agreed that we would try to correct some perspectives in the great canvas before us, didn´t we? Well, fire and brimstone, sheeps and muttons, light and darkness are definitely in the foreground now. Let us push them into the wings for the moment, agreed?

W: And what pieces are we having to put in their place, please?

B: Quite a few, and very convincing ones in my opinion. But for this we have to do some solid analyzing. And I am starting right away:

What we first have to do is to bring an order into the so-called evil. So many things and circumstances are labeled „evil" in our language that this word has become an uncritical synonym for everything we are afraid of, cannot control, sinister, bringing horror, damage and death. Out of this apparent chaos I am picking now the first category, the evil that comes to us by natural catastrophes.

When Lisbon was reduced to rubble by the earthquake which struck - of all days - on All Saints Day of 1755 the shock waves reverberated for a long time in the brilliant brains of that century, Voltaire for instance. Not everyone formulated the basic question as elegant as he did: why did God send this evil or let it happen? And more simple-minded people saw in that disaster the revengeful Jahve again who wanted to have atonement for sins compiled, evidently.

W: The list can be prolonged at will up to our times: earthquakes along the world´s belt of fire, cyclones drowning Bangla Desh, wildfire blackening half of Indonesia -

B: - and, tomorrow or in 10.000 years, a comet or meteorite head-on in a collision that will be the end of millions.

W: Well? Why does God, our Divine Power, let this happen? We have made no progress since Voltaire, have we?

B: Oh yes, we have, because we understand the workings of nature to the extent at least that nothing supernatural is any more in an earthquake or in the orbit of a comet. No revengeful or careless Divine Power has stoked the fire or planned a collision orbit. Certainly are the results each time „evil" for us, but you will agree that they lack any premeditation, a will to harm us.

W: Of course not, but this is not the point. The issue is: why is God letting this happen? If he is pre-scient, omniscient, and above all, if he loves us?

B: We are really at the decisive point here. In our earlier discussions we had put the question before us if God really wants to be all-knowing, in any phase or detail of an evolving universe. I want to confirm my answer in this context also: No, he does not, and there is no need for it.

W: And why not, please? Is a million or more human lives not need enough to avert a catastrophe?

B: The trouble with you is that you are seeing our planet as, if not the center, but as a preferred spot in the universe which has to be protected by the Divine Power from all natural disasters, correct?

W: Not totally, but in a way, yes. We have gained value, by natural evolution as well as by the revelation through Yeshua. Why should we be eliminated like an anthill under a tractor? It's not f a i r , this is the point I am trying to make, because we still believe that God, our Divine Power, would have the power to prevent it if so wanted, no? And especially, if the Divine Power is the personified love, as it was heard out of Yeshua?

B: Let us stay with the orbit of the big meteorite. He has been attracted by the gravity of our sun. The Divine Power is not changing fundamental laws of nature because we are begging her to do so. If she would do so in our case, then - for reasons of fairness - she would have to oblige billions of wishes of other intelligent habitats in the universe practically every terrestrial second. It is not difficult to foresee, even to our limited mind, that the universe would almost instantly become chaotic, meaning that a l l intelligent life would perish. So it´s practically we against the rest of the universe. How would you decide?

W: If the Divine Power would really decide, I have no more arguments. But is she? I think she is not taking any notice of our predicament! It just happens, under some natural, universal law - bang! Are we beloved creatures or are we not noticed at all?

B: I understand your sentiments, but isn´t your concept of God too small? There is no need for us to slip back into fatalism, if you really believe you are „in the hands" of the Divine Power in every nano-second of your bodily life.

The Islamic belief is giving us a fine example here. The believing Muslim, „he/she who has given him-/herself into the hand of God" has no difficulty to accept his end by a natural catastrophe without remonstrating with his God of the fairness or why thereof - because he/she knows that he/she is enshrouded in his love forever, with or without a terrestrial body.

W: I am still not reconciled to this view. But let us carry on. So far we have covered only one category of evil. What is the next one?

B: We are still with „evil" catastrophes, but this time they are man-made, not by natural laws. They occur where man is not able to control the technical world he has created: atomic plants melt down, planes crash, ships sink, trains collide - with hundreds or thousands of lives extinguished.

Again you will raise the question: an all-knowing God could have stepped in, preventing this evil? My answer to that is that the Divine Power has not planned or condoned this, not here on this planet nor in any other intelligent habitat - this would be the famous sin against the spirit - because it would mean that God is evil.

W: So you are debiting these man-made evils to the phenomenon of chance - by chance a plane falls down, right?

B: Not in the way that I would accord any selective power to „chance",
certainly not. The word „chance" has not received on objective
treatment by all high religions of this world, because it infers
something devious, contrary to a perfectly planned world in its
mechanistic sense - a spanner in the works, more or less.

They all overlooked that chance is the backside of the coin the face of
which reads „evolution". Evolution without chances, unprogrammed,
chaotic if you want, is impossible.

W: Stop here! This is now in flat contradiction to what we believe, that
evolution i s directed!

B: So we believe and have said it in an earlier section. „Direction"
however does not mean, or need, detail engineering.

The arrow of evolution points in the direction we believe, no doubt.
The „mechanism" of it, if this clumsy word is excused by you, is
dependent on chance.

W: And what is the „chance" that a plane falls down?

B: And what are the chances that you will reach the age of 85? You
should consult the mathematicians of the insurance companies, they
will show you their probability calculus -

W: This is not new to me. But their calculations are based on the number
of past events.

B: So what? All past plane crashes occured by chance also, if it was not
sabotage.

W: I give up. Also this category of evil is practically non-evil, correct?

B: I am glad that you see it this way now. If the Divine Power is admitting
the element of chance, she certainly does not position herself in the
role of a cosmic croupier who watches without feeling what bets are
on the table and then spins the ball. No. Her pronounced will is
evolution, and evolution includes chances - and also failures. Failures
with bitter, even „evil" consequences for individuals, families, nations,
whole planets!

I think we proceed now to the next category, right?

W: To the evil originating from sick human minds?

B: I would not limit it to our species. Let us hope that the beginning of reason came in an easier way in other habitats, that it did not cost millions of years of kill-before-you-get-killed.

W: But also this is evolution, or what else?

B: Definitely it is, but given the almost innumerable ways in which life could develop the chances are minimal in my opinion that this process was copied in many other habitats of the universe. Certainly it is not an optimum development which evolution would like to copy anyway. Of this I am sure.

W: Where do you take the courage from to say this? Without having the least knowledge of the existence, let alone the psychic pattern of another species in another habitat?

B: Well spoken. But I trust the opinion of the Spirit who talked from Yeshua. He did not have a very favourable opinion of our species, and he said so on various occasions: „Oh you depraved and unknowing bunch of beings! For how much longer do I have to stay with you, for how much longer must I endure you!" Remember these lines in the reports?
If we - and old Israel is seen as a representative of the world population only - if we were a species that is met quite often in the creation, spiritually, that is if we were a „representative" habitat dweller in the cosmos, he would have said it differently.

But no, he meant us as a specific product of evolution, with a highly doubtful potential of mutation to the better.

W: Thanks for the compliment. So man is evil since times immemorial, and every one of us carries the disease, the mark of Kain, the original sin? So the churches were ever right?

B: No way! You cannot hold it against these petrified organizations that they knew nothing of evolution until last century. But when they recognized it they battled the natural sciences to the hilt - and are far from being good loosers still today. So much for organizations who claim to have the Holy Spirit borrowed exclusively to them.

W: We have wandered away from our issue, it seems?

B: No, we are right in the middle of it. The mortgage of millions of terrestrial years which is contained in our older brain formations, inherited behaviour, is an awesome burden and we shall never shed it. But we shall be able to control it better with ongoing evolution and this act of control is already evolution.
But back to the original question: is it evil if a human being is crashing through the barriers of law, morals and education when he is driven by these primordial forces, which are still virulent in us: fear, hunger, sex, anger, defense of a perimeter?

W: It is certainly not good, but it is not evil in our sense. All nations of this world have come long since to the enlightened state of a penal law that makes a big difference between premeditated acts and those induced by the affectations you have cited; the difference between murder and manslaughter, for instance.

B: So it is, and therefore it is relatively easy to draw the line somewhere: In my understanding these animalistic acts must be punished, no doubt. But we cannot see them as an evil which is pervading the creation. But now we are coming closer to the core: what about the premeditated acts of evil committed by the human individual? Or by groups, masses, nations? Have we struck bottom now?

W: Indeed we do. We do not have to elaborate a sickness record beginning with child abuse and murder, blind acts of terrorism and finally arriving at the Holocaust of our century. In order to accentuate our horrors we tend to speak of „beasts" - or of the devils -

B: The comparison with beasts is an insult to every animal; the „devil" on the other hand is a very convenient excuse, because it makes the perpetrators of these crimes „obsessed", acting on higher orders, probably that of Satan itself -

W: Why „itself"? Himself!

B: I beg to disagree. The concept of evil has no gender, never had. But we reserve this for our last analysis, shall we?

W: Accepted. But what reason or probability speaks against the notion that an outer, evil force had taken command of the brains of the criminals, without their realizing it? They of course would reject any inference pointing to such a possibility. Now would that be not „devilish"?

B: If it really were so, it would not be demoniacal, but simply plain silly. Yes, you heard me right. I am referring again to Yeshua, where the reports say he was accused to expel evil spirits with the help of their supreme commander. Surely this must have been one of those moments where the Logos in Yeshua wanted to get rid of this place forever, and of this population. The warning of committing the sin against the Spirit, the ultimate insult against God, followed immediately.

W: You still have not disproved the possibly „devilish" acting of premeditating criminals.

B: The explanation is exactly in the place of the reports on Yeshua to which I just pointed. The Spirit from Yeshua gave it: any house divided in itself is doomed, so is any empire. If he, Yeshua, expelled the bad spirits in collusion with Satan, this would mean civil war in his empire. In other words: if there is an evil force at work that is beyond our understanding then this force cannot have as its strategic goal the annihilation of its subjects. This is why I said that it is plain silly to assume that Evil, with a capital letter, inflicts evil upon its followers.

W: Pol Pot managed to do just that. Without spiritual help from „outside!?

B: The millions he murdered were not his followers. They were helpless victims.

W: Granted. But one thing more: the reports on Yeshua state that he was expelling unclean spirits from stricken people. Some events are recorded in great detail, as e.g. the desolate father of a stricken boy pleads with him, or - a story which I still fail to understand - where the expelled spirits are granted another organic habitat in a big herd of swine, that commits suicide thereupon. The reports are not saying anything on whether the owners of the thousand-plus swine received any compensation?
If Yeshua says „evil spirits" to them and threatens them, and they are wailing not to be tormented by him - so how can we say that they are figments of imagination, or that the stricken people were mostly epileptics or just plain mad? Yeshua knew better, apparently! The Logos in him also had Satan as a very real spiritual power in his sights. He did not collide with him for the first time, and he said so clearly. Now what?

B: If I follow you then we are coming fast back to highly questionable cults of exorcism, voodoo, black masses and „the evil eye" which was enough to send its bearer to the stake, less than 400 years ago. I grant you that we are having an unexplained, unexplainable perhaps, phenomenon in the reports on Yeshua here. More on it we shall certainly not learn in this life, for sure.

But: my objection goes to the inference that the atrocities which our race has accumulated over the centuries are stemming, in their last essence, from „occupied" brains of leaders, their paragons or of the masses.

In my belief these evil events are man-made, from the sadistic butchering of children to the industrial-style gassing of Jews or any other forms of genocide. Man-made in the sense that they were not induced by the command of aliens who should watch gleefully over their accomplishments. No. I point to the pipe dreams of ideology, be it of religious or racial nature. I include the opium wars of economic despondency. I include the totalitarian systems of left and right, historic and neo-colonialism. They are evil, for sure. But it is not an imported evil. All of them are the result of either genetical defects in persons, the quest for hedonism in a decadent, sybaritic society, the fanaticism of ideologies or religions, dynastic or personal greed, naked power politics, perverted churches and, in the essence of it all, the absence of understanding, tolerance, respect and love between human beings -

W: - and the maximisation of profit, not to forget.

B: If it goes to the detriment of child welfare, ecology, reckless exploitation of not renewable resources, habitats of tribes, global climate factors - yes, very much so. In this sense also profits can be man-made „evil".

W: Which leaves us with the last category of evil in our view. And now I will take the lead, if you please:

We have repeatedly brushed aside the concept of evil which has its origin neither in evolution, nor in twisted human minds, but outside of our horizon of imagination. Certainly not as a cosmic principle, but truly existing in the parables of Yeshua. If we sum up the reports, it is a force directed against the Divine Power and the minds of those who have subscribed to her revelation.

B: The basic question is: was this power equivalent to the Divine Power when this cosmos came into being or is it the result of a spiritual sabotage later on?

W: The parable of the sower which the Logos in Yeshua gave was quite clear on this issue: the fiend came later, sowing weeds among the corn seeds.

B: And why did the Divine Power tolerate this? Again the problem of not practiced omni-science?

W: If you compare her to a farmer who is unaware of the doings of his fiendish neighbour - yes. But this is hardly the scenery we are talking about, isn´t it?
I am going back to the discussions we had in an earlier section, on the permanent revelation of the Divine Power and the free will of the beings who have attained reflexive thinking. We cannot work with a Gauss curve of normal distribution because we have no statistical data, how should we? So it is anybody´s guess to assume the percentages of habitats who have
a) accepted the revelation
b) rejected it
c) are just in the process of decision

But, just for driving in the nail somewhere, let us assume to be:
a) 30 per cent
b) 30 per cent
c) 40 per cent

The main tenets of the habitats who have rejected the revelation are:

− There is no Divine Power. The cosmos has been there forever and will continue to be so, steady state, expanding, pulsating - whatever.

− We see evolution at work. Within this framework, we have risen to the status of beings who not only have reflexive thinking, but were also able to shed our material vehicles. We are spiritual beings.

− We have given unto us a code of ethics that surpasses anything which the self-appointed messenger of a dubious Divine Spirit tried to preach us an unfathomable time ago.

- With the means available to us we have scanned our galaxy and the universe for other civilizations who correspond to our basic understanding and we have found them, which is very comforting indeed. We are on the right track. We constantly communicate.

- We register acutely the activities of intelligent civilizations who are adoring a Divine Power. Out of our free will, which is a product of evolution, we have decided that there is no need for a Divine Power in order to explain our being and this cosmos.

- We shall go on to inform those civilizations accordingly inspite of the fact that we have been received in a hostile attitude sometimes in the habitats where we started. In one of them they denounce us as „devils" - whatever that may be, as an „anti-force" to the Divine Power they are paying homage to, as „dangerous" to their existence, in whatever form, which we clearly are not.

B: It is a very likely presentation - but without any proof. Therefore we have to discard it, I am afraid.

W: Don´t do it too early. Because, as members of a population that embraced the revelation through Yeshua we are still under a persistent, though not noticeable information attack.

B: I want to put it more simple and more gripping: above our heads, apparently, there is a battle raging, nothing less, without body counts or devastated habitats. It is a great pity and misunderstanding that the forces who are proclaiming a universe without Divine Power have been dismissed by us as „devils" and „evil". In their own sense, they are certainly not „evil". They think of themselves as an alternative, and a very viable one indeed, of constructing and maintaining an order of the universe that is understandable, effective, fair, working for all habitats that reach reflexive thinking in its evolutionary course, and then, now comes the big switch:

> to give evolution a new arrow,
> establishing liveable, spiritual, ethical,
> lawful habitats which offer their
> subscribers a meaningful, interesting
> existence, devoid of sorrow, crime, fear -
> for the period of the calculable universe,

(B):   - in short: a life of beauty, bliss and secured spiritual existence until this cosmos exists. Eternally for the steady-state believers. Quite sufficiently eternal for the believers in a pulsating universe. But: no need for a Creator or a Divine Spirit!

W: All this is very impressive, but tell me one thing: Is this power, that we call Divine, ready and willing to give spiritual battle to this strategy? For what should it fight against expect for the fact that she is the Supreme Being, the creator of this universe and that she holds the keys to the future? If she is accepting the principle of free will in her creation then she also has to accept a universal resistance movement, isn´t it?

B: Yes. And this is just the point we were making in our analysis: Also a „Satan" as a sum of all cosmic forces directed against the evolution as planned by the Divine Spirit is not „evil" in the traditional human sense, regardless of the sometimes ridiculous paintings of past centuries.

W: But what will happen to this movement at the end of this universe?

B: For this we have reserved the following section of this chapter.

Doomsday, And Then ?

W: When we are talking about the end of the world as it is given by the Logos in Yeshua we end up in bewilderment. In his famous end-of-time scenario we see a mixture of events; one of them clearly happened about 40 years after his death, the devastation of Jerusalem under the Roman emperor Titus, as narrated by Flavius Josephus. Then other horrible events are telescoping into each other as if it were an unending string of ever increasing torments without a spell of relief in between them.

B: And what happens to evolution? Or are these events part of the cosmic evolution? Are they heralding the breakdown and end of the cosmos, evolution and all included? And, mind you, the predictions of the Apocalypsis Joannis are still more nasty in comparison. The term „overkill" has its roots directly there!

W: When we decided to do this book we agreed that we would consider only the four reports on Yeshua as a still acceptable basis, regardless of their contradictions and of the additions of later scribes. The apocalypse however is a vision, partly grandiose, partly a horror scenario. The telescoping effect is there again as in the eschatology speech from Yeshua. At any rate, the impressions eluded the vocabulary of the seer, as they would ours today. How could it be otherwise if a multi-dimensional world confronts a representative of our four-dimensional possibilities? So, the apocalypse stays out. What we have to do, however, is again to analyze the options: possible doomsday scenarios scale by scale: terrestrian, solar, galactic and cosmic, and to compare each time the words from Yeshua with the physics of each.

B: I also think that this is the best way to get in some sound probabilities. May I start?

W: By all means, do.

B: Let us begin with our good old planet. He is roughly 4 billion years old and evolution is still in full swing on it. By what would he, and only he, be doomed?

W: Well, one possible and man-made origin has been lifted with the end of the Cold War. This limits the possibilities to external reasons only, e.g. the collision with a comet or a giant meteorite, as we have discussed already.

B: One man-made cause, however, is still existing: we could poison our planet to the extent that organic life, including us, is threatened as a whole.

W: As of today we do not seem to be very far off this point, do we?

B: All right, accounted for. But let us revert to the four reports: would the forces of the heavens be shaken, would suns plunge from heavens? Applicable?

W: Not in the least. The demise of our planet, in whatever form, would be a local catastrophe of sheer unimportance to the cosmos. So, what is the next step?

B: It is our solar system. First we take the measuring rod of the natural scientists and state that radiation pressure and gravity will balance our sun´s existence for the next 4 to 5 billion years. After using up most of her fission fuel her burning diameter will balloon, she will become a Red Giant which burns the whole planetary system to ashes. Afterwards, because of her mass, she will not explode as a nova but will slowly extinguish and be a cold ball of matter for the rest period of this cosmos.

W: 4 billion years are a very comforting period for us, isn´t it? We, our human race, will be lucky if it will have an evolutionary life of, say, 50 million years. Yes, why should we be more modest than the dinosaurs?

B: Jokes aside: is this scenario matching the doomsday lines in the four reports? In my opinion not in the least. It will be the death of one solar system of which we have billions in our galaxy. In other words: again a local catastrophe with repercussions neither on the galactic nor on the cosmic level.

W: So we go one step further. Do you remember when we studied the foto of the remote galaxy that is torn apart in its middle by an explosion for which our physicists have no explanation? Their only concept is that the density of matter within the galaxy reached a critical value.

B: The Hubble telescope of recent times has done better than that. Do you recall this breathtaking picture of the two colliding galaxies in „Antennae"? I have never seen something as grandiose and awe-inspiring in my life. And now let us get out the texts of the doomsday speech from Yeshua again, whether they fit in this scenario: Are the forces of heavens shaken for the unlucky inhabitants of these galaxies?

W: Oh yes, and how!

B: Will the sun lose its shine and will the stars fall from the heavens?

W: Yes, literally. Billions of them!

B: Now we are out of the fog, finally. One scenario the Logos described was the cataclysma of a world, very much so, because a galaxy like ours certainly is a world in itself. It is of no importance that the „process" of this doom does not happen in seconds but needs millions of years, and starts with definite and understandable warnings. But the event is spreading out with inexorable momentum - a farewell to millions of habitats having reached evolutionary heights far above ours, or like ours, or who were on the way to it - finis!

W: So: a punishment to sinful, godless creatures?

B: This is the way the so-called christian churches had it since Paul confirmed the bizarre and most un-christian concept of pre-determination.

W: We do not know, however, how galaxies usually end. Is this violent finale the rule or the exception thereof? We are fairly sure today that there is a Black Hole at the center of a spiral galaxy - but how should we know more? At any rate, just to ram this point home, it is not the punishment of the Divine Spirit, and it is not the end of the cosmos as a whole. It is certainly more than just a local catastrophe compared to the end of our solar system, but still the cosmos is going on inspite of it.

B: Which leaves us with the last grand option, right?

W: Yes, and the more I thought of it the more I became convinced that the Logos in Yeshua was not announcing the death of our galaxy. An exploding or colliding galaxy is such an enormous event that it eludes formulas and vocabulary. It corresponds to elements of the doomsday speech from Yeshua, yes, but not on a universal scale.

If you take the end of this cosmos, however, as it is understandably drawn by the astrophysicists who subscribe to the model of a pulsating universe, then this, and only this scenario is the backdrop against the eschatology speech from Yeshua. The scientific partisans of a steady-state or ever increasing universe, of course, smile upon this notion. I do n o t smile upon it, but for another reason, and that is the justice of the Divine Power. Justice in the way that every habitat that developed reflexive thinking must have had its chance to opt for her revelation or for the spiritual movement we discussed in the last section.

B: But we are convinced that evolution is going on in all those habitats, also in those of the dissenters?

W: This is one of our central tenets, yes.

B: But when new stars are born all the time, as we can observe now via Hubble, then also new habitats of intelligent life will be formed over the eons again - do you think that the Creator will cut in somewhere, drawing the line regardless of how many promising habitats are developing at that point?

W: You put the Creator in the role of a sculptor who is growing more and more dissatisfied with what he produced and finally, in a fit of rage, he is smashing everything, ready statues and torsos alike. No, not so. We, who believe in a Creator, do believe also that he has given this cosmos a begin and an end. There is nothing sinister about the end, because we can safely assume already with our present knowledge that the energy of an imploding cosmos is, at the same time - or timeless state - the Big Bang of the next cosmos.

B: It is important to state, from our point of view, that the end of the present cosmos is roughly calculable since Mr. Hubble detected the „exploding" universe seventy years ago. Gravity will put the brakes on this momentum to a standstill, and from there the reverse process will accelerate, until the matter of the universe re-unites in the mathematical point of energy for which we have only the flippant expression „Big Bang".

W: This is today´s most probable scenario. On the other hand, our scientists are still searching for the „dark matter" in the universe, which must be there theoretically - but to no avail.

B: I think that our race will be in for many surprises within the next thousand years or so, about the structure of the universe. But this is not the point of our discussion. What we have put in the foreground is that the end of our observable cosmos has been programmed already in the lightning of its birth. There is no disappointed Creator who overthrows his creation. There is not, above all, the revengeful Jahve of Hebrew times, awaiting us in a cul-de-sac at the end of time, with no possibility of escape.

W: It is high time now that we are also discussing our individual trial that we have to face after bodily death and finally that grand trial which the Logos in Yeshua has canvassed „at the end of Time".
I am starting, if you please.
We believe in the essence of the revelation through Yeshua that our personality will go on living after our bodily death, in spiritual form. We also believe that we have to render an account of our short terrestrial life. We know from the four reports against what categories we shall be measured. We also have a good idea about who will do the measuring: the Logos who was in Yeshua. We also have reason to believe that the outcome of this trial will be decisive for the „quality" of the life awaiting us -

B: Sorry, stop here, please, I do not agree! Here we are at a crucial point. Do you mean to say that the pattern of a human life which spans some responsible 60 years should be decisive for an eternity?

W: We have agreed that we would discuss the concept of eternity in the last section of this chapter, no?

B: Eternity or 10^{40} terrestrial years, what does it matter? The point is that, in the worst case, this spiritual personality can be sentenced to suffer agonizing spiritual pain until the „end of time"?

W: The Logos in Yeshua was very clear on this issue.

B: 60 years of malice on earth against 10^{40} years of despair - do you call this fair?

W: I am not subscribing to your figures, but I also do not think that this is compatible with a Divine Spirit who not only has, but is, love. But - there it is in the reports, we cannot hide it.

B: Imagine that this spiritual world is really constructed as it is given in the Lazarus parable. Here - we. There - they. And no contact is possible. Taken together the Divine Power is creating a cosmic zoo of wailing and desperate spiritual beings, to be watched with relish from the blessed side - I tell you, if this were true then I would ask the Divine Power to eliminate, extinguish me without remembrance in this very moment, because I shall not bear to witness this cosmic atrocity.

W: There is no escape clause in this contract, meaning that the individual has no option to cancel himself out forever, not to remember and not to be remembered. At least this minimum mercy should be extended by a loving God, even if he cannot bear the spiritual presence of a depraved personality.

B: On a universal scale we have the same black-or white judgement again in the great finale of which the Spirit in Yeshua speaks. Sheep to the right, muttons to the left - and then? Perennial bliss on the right, everlasting sorrow and pain on the left? This cannot be! All the more so since the final reckoning is done with the cosmic resistance movement of which we talked. They exercised their free will but lost. Vae victis? On purpose I am not using the phrasings of the four reports who cannot hide a certain sadistic satisfaction on the fate that has been prepared for the God-less. The same unforgiving attitude you can read also from the Koran when it is dealing with these last matters. With one exception only: in the Koran we read that those, for whom nobody pleaded mercy, are indeed fed to the flames eternally - if God should not decide otherwise! So the Muslim belief is far more gracious in this question than the Judaic-Christian scenario.

W: So what will be at the end of time? A spiritual cosmic holocaust watched by jubilant victors?

B: No. In my belief there will be a General Pardon by the Divine Power.

W: Are you having the slightest information or probability on this daring opinion?

B: Yes, very much so. A Divine Power who has accorded free will to her creation will be able to tolerate also a negative attitude towards her, if otherwise these spiritual entities employed kindness and mercy among themselves and to others. They were very near to her all the time without knowing it. So why should they be punished, and eternally at that? God is love.

W: And what about the scenarios of the four reports? What about the Stalins, Hitlers, Torquemadas, Himmlers, Albas, Pol Pots and their helpers?

B: To these first: I hope that they will get their chance to disappear forever. To the reports: I seriously doubt whether the Logos talking from Yeshua was omniscient. This was confirmed when he acknowledged through Yeshua that also he does not know the hour and day of the cosmic cataclysm, only the „Father". How, then, could he be so sure of a Jahve battlefield at the end of times instead of a General Pardon? Perhaps he knew many other things also not in their last consequence? This is my explanation of the merciless texts of the four reports on this issue.

Eternity - How Much Of It ?

W: A judgement of our personality will be, after we leave our terrestrial hull behind. But we expect this to happen as a necessary part of the „breathtaking" - if we still had one - transition, for which we have only the sullen word „death" in store. Or do we have to wait until Doomsday, quite literally, for our re-appearance? The four reports are very ambiguous about that question.

B: I do not think that the contradictions of the reports help us to any deeper or higher foreboding. The essence of the event has been „buried", quite literally, under the pompe funèbre which is draped over the whole happening on the one side. On the other, venerable but at the same time doubtful texts are read over the dead body: Blessed are those who die in the Lord because they can rest from their toil. Or the still more misleading terms of „eternal sleep" or „eternal peace", inferring either a total inactiveness of the personality after its transition or a universal waiting limbo of „deep-frozen" personalities who will be activated at the sound of the final trumpet.

W: Let me ask you directly: do you think that the dead are dead?

B: Not for a second! Their material hull will be reduced to its final natural elements and no matter how, down to the possibility of being digested by a white shark - sorry for the example, but I want to make the argument stick!

Their personality, as we have discussed at the resurrection point, will have a spiritual form of which we cannot fantasize. Who believes in the revelation through Yeshua believes also in this form of life to come. Not only we, but all habitats who accept the revelation.

W: One of the most distorting facts is in my opinion the latent fear of boredom in eternity. Nobody admits it, everybody has it. Or are you satisfied with the prospect of eternal bliss? Even such an arcane situation will become stale after a while, isn´t it? Eternally pampered, protected, cuddled - I am not sure whether my personality could endure this very long - certainly not for an eternity!

B: You are haughty and arrogant, my friend! If you are applying the usual concepts of earthly bliss to the state of being we shall - hopefully - attain then your God simply is too small. And we are doing this book to say that the Divine Power is not to be harnessed in texts, liturgy, cults, commandments, organizations nor by any priest! Do you want to give up our project?

W: I think I deserved that cold shower. But you will not deny that opinions like these are rampant, or?

B: That´s just the pity of it, but you were in good companionship for a while. If you recall the eternal bliss that is promised to the faithful Muslimin, the male half of it at least, then you are back to the pampering scenario. The Koran is notoriously silent in this context on what the female half could expect, by the way.

W: I am sure that no modern muslim would adhere to these awkward notions of beatitude today. They also think that they are allegoric, chosen for lack of a more moving vocabulary, no?

B: Now you are treading dangerous ground. We agreed in our list of contents that we would analyze the situation of Islam in the next chapter, and not only that, that we would establish some trend lines there. I propose that we leave it at that. Here, in this discussion, the answer to your remark is: Yes, for the modern muslim; a clear no for the fundamentalist muslim, and both are literally at daggers today over the explosive question whether the Koran can be interpreted at all, notably so whether parts are allegoric or not. The pendulum is currently swinging very far to the fundamentalists, for a mixture of reasons, and we are experiencing the first storm gusts. The thunderstorm is yet to come.

W: We were also drawn away a little from our central topic: how much of eternity is in store for us? Whether it will be „digestible" - I apologize for this question!

B: Forget it. I want to make my central point in this discussion: All concepts of eternity, be they venerable or of less imagination, suffer from the assumption that eternity is a period of endless, indefinite time, „as time goes by", but never. And there, admittedly or not, we feel anxiety: what to do, or still worse: what nothing to do in eternity? The basic mistake on the whole concept is that time will still exist for us after transition. This is not so. There will be no time any more, we shall not experience a past, a now, a future. We simply shall be.

W: Are you having any good probability on what you were just saying?

B: Yes, if you read the lines in one of the four reports where the Logos in Yeshua is smashing to pieces the sexual notions of the Sadducees in their „one woman - seven brothers" story. In order to be understandable he had to choose the comparison of the personalities in transition state to that of angels - because this was still something they could fantasize somehow.

W: But I am challenging your theory! You were saying that there will be no more time in this state of being. If you were referring to the closure of the cosmos as a whole, as we saw it in our previous chapter, then, and only then, time would come to an end. To this I agree. If I or you are dead, or transformed, if you like this better, this solar system, this galaxy and this cosmos will still go on in its evolution unperturbed, in space a n d t i m e !

B: What I am saying now has no support in the four reports whatsoever and please do not see it as an Houdini trick to bow out of the discussion: since you are right in what you just said the only result that appears still logical to me is that transition does not only mean a change of place and of state of being, but a state of being that is not any more connected with the space-time-continuum of our universe.

W: Another universe then? A final Super-Universe? The multiverse of some scientists?

B: We don´t know, we cannot fantasize. It is totally out of reach for our present capacity of imagination, let alone reason.

Chapter III:

DIRECTION

Plotting The Course

W: In the first chapter we looked back without regrets. In the second we looked up quite courageously. In the third one we will look confidently ahead now, isn´t it?

B: Yes, the question is only: how far, for how long?

W: I think that we have a very natural border waiting for us. This will be the line across which we are not seeing any satisfying probabilities of development any more -

B: What do you mean by „development"?

W: The spiritual development of our funny race, or call it „increasing cognitive ability", if this sounds better to you?

B: No, I like the term „development" very much, because for me it is the synonym of evolution, seen over a tiny time distance. But what exactly do we want to cover?

W: The fate of the churches in the foreseeable future, for once.

B: And what is „foreseeable"?

W: As I said already, until no more viable probabilities are coming in, for better or for worse. We are witnessing a status quo of them today which we consider fossilized. Now we have to debate what their future will be in the light of our second chapter.

B: Do you think that their command structures have a chink in the armour somewhere so that renegade opinions like ours may infiltrate?

W: If I am answering now we shall pre-empt the first section already. Please wait a little.

B: At any rate we have to include Islam here also, even if it is not a hierarchy church.

W: Include in the chapter, yes, but in a section of its own, because clouds are forming over that religion, not only for the Muslimin, but for the entire world.

B: Agreed. So we have two sections nailed already.

W: Since we are very down-to-earth again in this chapter I would go one step further, looking into the probability of the chaos that will result by the demise of organized churches, in short: whether the revelation through Yeshua has a chance to survive.

B: And the end of this chapter, my friend, shall be radiant with joy, talking about the serenity, drive and impact of a belief in the revelation that is no more geocentric, once and for all, but evolutionary!

W: Now, now! We agreed in the beginning that we would do no proselytizing. To this we keep.

B: If we cannot convey this deep satisfaction to our readers which we are experiencing we have served only dry food for thought. I want to say also something about the taste of this food!

W: Which is purely personal!

B: Of course it is, what else? But it can be shared, if so wanted.

W: Your are set on it already, so go ahead!

The End Of Priest-Run Churches

W: Remember the sunday one year ago when we decided to write down the essence of our discussions?

B: How should I forget this day with all the headaches it has given me, and more to come!

W: The trigger to our decision were the bells of the two churches down in that village. Two churches are necessary in a community of, say, 2.000 people to pray to the same God, different bells of course, different priests, liturgy, books of prayer.

B: This led us straight to our discussion on the manifest atrophy of the so-called christian churches. Are you still subscribing to that?

W: Very much so, and not only that. Only we did not think wide and far enough on this occasion. This pattern of agony does not only apply to the so-called christian churches or sects, but to all priest-dominated churches of this planet, of every denomination. Or call them religious hierarchy organizations, if you like this better, spanning from the Dalai Lama over the Shinto church, the Jewish Rabbinate, the Mormons, national protestant churches to the Vatican.

They suffer from diverse sicknesses, but one of them has befallen them all and is suffocating them: it is their priests who hold the keys to heaven. Nobody can bypass them on the desired path. They, of course, see this differently. They are the spiritual leaders, guides, shepherds, wise men and what not. Above all, however, their claim is of supernatural origin and cannot be questioned, therefore. And the last rest of individualism among their flock went to pieces when the churches or sects closed ranks with the secular powers - which they still do today, but not any more for the persecution of disbelievers, but for the sheer survival of their organizations.

B: I hate to cut in, Walter, but apparently you are working yourself into a cold fury. This is understandable but fury is a dubious escort in any discussion. May I propose the analytical approach instead: we are filtering out the common strains of bacteria in priest-run churches. Two we have mentioned already, this is their claim of exclusivity and the cozying up to the secular powers. What else have we?

W: Priests, or whatever their name is, consider themselves as the exclusive administrators and dispensers of supernatural blessings, sacraments. The mystery character that is draped around the fact plus an awe-inspiring liturgy cements this claim.

B: The next bacterium is not less mean: priests decide whether an individual can become a member of the organization, nobody else.

W: Priests are paid for their services, in whatever form, be it merciful rice in the bowls of Asian monks or opulent civil service salaries in Germany, Austria and Switzerland. In short: their believers sustain them, because their duties apparently do not allow any bread-earning activity besides.

B: This is relatively harmless in contrast to the next item: priests, in all ages, in every system, have tried to spiritually dominate government and society. They cannot exercise any more their power plays as e.g. in the Egyptian culture or in the Middle Ages of Europe. The aim is still there, only the methods are more refined today.

The nuisance of a Vatican State is still acknowledged by most governments of this world, the last absolutist monarchy on earth and its most prominent priest-church fossil. National churches, on the other hand, know exactly on which side their bread is buttered and do not risk clashes with the secular power which leaves them with inherited wealth, tax privileges and the possibility of increased fortune by matrons'testaments.

W: Do you know, for instance, that the catholic and protestant church in Germany, taken together, are the biggest land-owners there, after the state property?

B: Small wonder if today's governments feel that they have to respect donations made by kings or emperors thousand years ago. Land was abundant and cheap at that time.

W: But the abbeys and monasteries were also bulwarks against the tide of aggressors, this should not be forgotten, no?

B: This is taken from the history textbooks when we were children. No onslaught ever was stopped by them, how could it be? Christianization was the word, and once this was accomplished by fire and sword then the church stepped in, forcing the now christian labour slaves to lay down forests and to till the earth they did not own, but which the church did.

W: In order to be fair it must be mentioned, however, that the caritative work by the priest churches is still very welcome today, or not?

B: Running soup kitchens is an act of mercy, no doubt. But this never infringed on the substance of wealth which the priest churches amassed. Do you know that the two richest dioceses of the Catholics, Chicago and Cologne, are rated by financial experts to have a net worth of one billion dollars?

Or do you remember the out-of-court settlement which the Vatican struck up with the consortium of international banks who were induced by the „Istituto degli opere religiose" - Vatican Bank - to entrust large deposits to the Banco Ambrosiano in Milan, Mr. Calvi? The settlement cost the Vatican 500 million dollars!

And now I am coming to the caritative institutions you have mentioned. Of course their services are welcome, both by the poor and sick and by the government. But do you realize that they are only stepping in for unable governments? Because it is the prime obligation of governments, not of church organizations, to tend to the poor and the sick. Unable or unwilling governments, from city administrations to state level, are certainly grateful for the relief which caritative church institutions are bringing.

On the other hand we see e.g. in Germany that caritative church organizations are employed by the public bodies - and paid - just like any other private organization in this field. But now we have gone astray a little bit from our central issue.

W: We said that priest churches are doomed to die. Where is our direct proof?

B: In history. You can take the whole spectrum: Mesopotamia, Egypt, Persia, Israel, Greece, Rome, and also the druids, if you want to. Whenever a religious belief was governed exclusively by priests and the hierarchy they were developing it did not survive. The main reason invariably was the rift that they started in proclaiming themselves as supernaturally ordained, knowing and of high status therefore, whilst their subjects were barred from direct access to their deities, unknowing, laymen, laywomen.

(B): The rift widened as the church organizations became rich and also secular powers. At the height of their secular power all of them failed, especially the Catholic church, to establish a secular order that would have earned the title „humanitarian", let alone the love-thy-neighbour level. Instead, we had inquisition, slave trade and the genocide in Latin America.

W: I want to point out in this context that some high beliefs in history like the teachings of Kung-fu-tse, Lao-tse, Buddha, and also Islam never needed priests - and are still flourishing.

B: With the exception of Islam, I agree. This monolith is showing different fissures than the so-called christian churches, but enough of them to be deeply worried.

W: I am coming in from another angle. Unable or perverted organizations as the so-called christian beliefs may be in their majority, they still have as their common core, or heritage, the revelation through Yeshua. We believe in the Logos that spoke from him. Would the Logos tolerate that these organizations, with all their warts and hunchbacks, will fizzle out like a candle in the wind? They are „his" churches still, no?

B: I know this form of self-consolation from countless dictums of their hierarchy! They have not made mistakes in the past, they say, maybe they have created misunderstandings, such as the process of Galilee or an inquisition. Mistakes are out, since they are governed at all times by the Holy Spirit. And he, they say, will steer them through all accusations and their protagonists will take exercises in demure suffering at the hands of the mud-slinging, godless crowd - but their ship will never capzise. I am tempted to add: as long as they have the welcome ballast of wealth on its keel, their outward life is far longer than without it.

And the much-cited Holy Spirit, which of course is claimed exclusively by them, has left them in disgust not only when their stakes were burning but probably since Paul literally condemned all non-believers.

W: I agree. So what is called for? To wait generations until the atrophy of the priest organizations has reached a state where governments are inclined to give the coup-de-grace to the organization? Or in the case of the so-called christian churches, should the believers in the revelation through Yeshua start a revolt against their shepherds?

B: I hope that they will not make this mistake. Spiritually, yes, by all means. There the thing to do is: dry them out, leave the organization. But never, never take recourse to force! This would be more than a crime, it would be a mistake, to cite a famous historic line.

First of all, the secular governments would not look on idly to law-breaking acts, rioting, destroying church property or harming priests, monks, nuns.

Secondly, the organizations would automatically be in the role of martyrs and underdogs earning a corresponding, if small, sympathy bonus.

Thirdly, there are international contracts to be observed, even with such an anachronism as the Vatican State. In Germany each federal state has its own „Konkordat" with the Vatican, for historical reasons. Contracts can be given notice to, however, they need not be torn up and be declared non-valid ex tunc. No, all this must go gentleman-like, and it will be all the more deadlier so. For if the organizations have become dry riverbeds, every government will ask them whom they are representing besides their staff?

W: You are saying that the decision will be done on the political level ultimately?

B: Yes, and this will lead to a critical polarization of the respective country. The church organizations, with their back to the wall, will preach Holy War, naturally. But it will depend on the evolutionary level of the people whether they can make a distinction then between the revelation and its ill-fated, perverted administrators. All political parties who still will have a „C" in their logo, for „christian", will rally around the dying churches. I can hear already the rhetoric of „occidental apocalypse, harakiri of a whole civilization etc. etc.". And, mind you, this could really turn into civil war, where formerly peaceful neighbours slit each others´throats over this issue. This danger is absolutely imminent, I should say.

W: So what are we distilling from this scenario? That priest churches are in spiritual, but not in economic agony the world over? That as long as they are allowed to keep their historically amassed wealth the danger of dying from spiritual asphyxiation is less acute than if they were poor organizations. Further: the governments are in danger if they start to dismantle the organizations, stripping them of their privileges, confiscating their estates.

B: A good resumé. So the best way for all would be if these organizations would declare spiritual bankruptcy themselves, handing the administration to their laymen/laywomen, abdicating from all concepts and paraphernalia of secular power, asking their flock and the world for forgiveness for all the blood and tears they have brought on over the centuries, or where they looked the other way in holocausts - practically a spiritual and economic liquidation of the total organization. Is this a probability?

W: It is, but so remote that it borders on zero.

B: So the end of priest-run churches under a conflict situation is more probable?

W: For me it is a certainty. Whether the conflict will be a bloodless one depends on the evolutionary level of the population.

B: Are you daring any time prognostics?

W: In the reverse way, yes. I would be very surprised if the first national so-called christian church organization would go into liquidation before three or four generations from now. But it will not take much more time after that, I am sure.

B: And on the non-christian priest churches?

W: I think that they will take longer to die. My reason for this assumption is that e.g. in the Japanese Shinto church or in Buddhism and Hinduism there is a generally much stronger interaction between the believers and the priests than is the case with the so-called christian beliefs, where history has eroded the trust between the two. So these organizations will hang on more toughly until they give themselves up. I am not venturing to put a time tag on this, however.

B: To sum it up, how are priest-run churches to be ended?

W: Always against their will, not by revolutions - and soon, hopefully.

Islam In Contorsion

B: We have said on earlier occasions that Islam, world-wide, is heading into a major upheaval. With whom will it collide?

W: With itself, and not only once, but twice. For once, with its own spiritual history from where it is haunted more than ever by evolutionary forces which were forcibly suppressed one thousand years ago and are coming back with a vengeance now. The second earthquake in Islam, the comparison is very fitting, I think, will result from social revolutions in the so-called Islamic democracies; the first storm gusts are whizzing around our ears since years, but the world has shrugged them off - so far.

B: You are referring to the Islamic fundamentalists?

W: Yes. Until now in 1997, we have 30.000 people massacred in Algeria since the stupid cancellation of the elections which put the fundamentalists into power - on paper.

We have the Talibans in Afghanistan who try to roll the country back spiritually by more than a thousand years. We have a regime in Iran that sentences a young German to death by stoning because he dared to love a Muslim maiden. But all this is the veneer only. If we want to present an understandable pattern we have to do two things: first, we have to describe in what the true Muslim believes, what is expected of him by the Koran. Secondly, we must make an excursion into Islamic history to a period which, as I said, is not only haunting but shaking the religious monolith again now. The cracks on it are apparent. There are only two imaginable scenarios for the future. We will discuss them in detail.

B: I know that you have lived for some years in an Islamic country, so please take the lead.

W: Thank you. Of course I got interested in their faith, philosophy, history. I daresay that I know the Koran better than two thirds of all Muslimin. But I want to start out into my canvas by describing what fascinated me from the very first day on, and still does so: when at high noon, e.g. in bustling Cairo, the call to prayer is blared from the minarets then the man walking in front of me in a western business suit is putting down his briefcase on the pavement, draws out a handkerchief, kneels on it and starts to pray - and not only he, but most of the milling crowd also, forming nice ranks of ten or twelve abreast, depending on the width of the road, one row after another if you gaze ahead or back - this is something which no so-called christian belief was ever able to accomplish. It is simply great, moving, and very evolutionary. The believer needs no priest, bishop, pope, elders, self-appointed prophets, shamans - whatever - to give reverence to his one God - Allah.

B: I know it only by photographs and television, where the lines of the faithful, thousands in one Mosque yard, are praying. Yes, to witness this must be very impressive.

W: We must go to an Islamic country together. This will be a lasting memory for you.

B: But you only started into our theme with a momentary glimpse, a snapshot.

W: Are you having patience with me if I make a swing into history?

B: If you don´t become too professorial, it´s fine with me.

W: You can kick my shinbone any time you feel that I get carried away. So, let´s see now. Yes, the best thing to start with is the „normal" Muslim. What is his essence of belief? For once, it is the Koran. The Koran is the total of divine revelations that were opened to Mohammed. We have only his word for it. We find Abraham, Moses and Yeshua in the surahs, more of the so-called Old Testament than in the four reports on Yeshua. These three, Mohammed points out, also spoke the word of God. In case of contradictions he claims preference, of course.

Now, what is the credo of a faithful Moslem? He believes in angels, heaven, demons, hell, resurrection of the soul a n d the body, predestination, Last Judgement, and life everlasting for the accepted and the rejected beings.

B: I have read that the Muslim has certain tasks on this earth, no?

W: Yes, exactly five of them: to obey the five prayer times per day; to give alms; to obey the fasting during Ramadan; to do the pilgrimage to Mecca at least once in his life; and to believe in Allah and his prophet, Mohammed.

B: I have always looked to the commandment of fasting in the Muslim world with a twinkle in my eye. I shudder in disgust at the memory of the „christian" fanatical pillar saints of Syria. I declare my veneration for Mahatma Ghandi, however, when he declared to fast to death when the faith riots went rampant in the divided sub-continent.

The Ramadan fasting of the Muslimin, however, is in my opinion an anti-fasting. Where, please, is the spiritual gain of not eating, not drinking during daylight if you are allowed to browse through the tables at your will after sunset? Of course I am glad that this is so, otherwise the Muslim world would take months afterwards to recover from a rigid fasting. But where is evolution in that, can you tell me?

W: In Ramadan fasting there is none, for sure. But we are being distracted. Islam had no need for priests, or church, or hierarchy. What the faithful needed was somebody who would lead them in prayer and give a sermon on lines of the Koran or the Hadith.

B: Hadith? Please explain!

W: Besides the Koran there grew an oral tradition of sayings, happenings, miracles, yes, and - you can call it background formation of a faith - that took its roots in Mohammed himself and also in the people around him. Of course this collecion went out of control very early so that an eminent scholar, Al-Bokhari, was entrusted to do a purified version of the Hadith, around 870. If we believe his contemporaries, he examined about 500.000 verses and boiled them down to 7275, those where a direct and proven linkage to Mohammed or his early followers could be established. And this is the Sunna of today ,hence the Sunnite half of Islam. The Shia, hence: Shiites, developed over the fight whether Ali and Hussain, both murdered, were the legitimate successors of the Prophet instead of the Caliphs. This split is still going through Islam today, after 1.200 years. But it is not the split by which Islam is going to explode in the near future.

B: I cannot expect to become an expert of Islam in five minutes. So thank you for a very interesting backdrop, but could you come to the core of our issue now, please?

W: I beg your pardon, but I think that all this was necessary for the following:

The salient point is that Islam never had a reformation worth its name in its history. As with any new belief there were sects galore in the centuries following Mohanned's death, among them also very sympathetic ones, e.g. the Murjites, who preached that no Moslem could everlasting be damned. There were others, less inviting: the Jabrites, who denied free will and preached predestination, sharply opposed by the Quadarites, who confirmed free will - and, and, and.

But when Islam had time to think instead of conquering more territory from Cordoba to Damascus, it ran into the Greek philosophers, notably so into Aristotle, which was quite intoxicating food, especially his „Organon".

Now the orthodox Islam still holds today that the Holy Koran had always existed in the mind of Allah, only its revelation was an event in space and time of our planet. The original, so to say, is not accessible, and - now we come to the dynamite - is not to be changed.

The Mutazilites, means: Secessionists, were begging to differ, around the year of 757. They denied the eternity of the Koran, with all respect for the holy book. But, they said, where the Koran or the Hadith contradicts human reason and experience, then they must be interpreted in or by allegorics, i.e. as venerable but nebulous circumscriptions of unfathomable events. Against these, the Mutazilites put „kalam", which means logic, the effort to reconcile reason and faith.

In a truly evolutionary effort they cleaned away all terrestrial notions of Allah. They were right in maintaining that he had no hands, feet, anger, repentance or hatred - and that he could never be insulted by his created beings.

B: This is truly evolutionary! There is no parallel in the so-called christian beliefs of this time.

W: Thomas Aquinas was 400 years off from this Islamic stage - and he twisted his Aristotle in a way for which we, in retrospect, have the almost insulting word „scholastic" in store.

B: Carry on, please! What happened to the Mutazilites? Why was there no lasting reformation?

W: Because of the mistake which many rulers have made throughout history: to declare their newly found, honest belief to be the state religion.

B: Oh, oh. I smell disaster, Carry on, please!

W: The Mutazilites flourished under the Caliphs Al-Mansoor, Haroon Al-Rashid, yes, the one from 1001 nights, and Al-Mamoon. And he was the one who decreed this faith to be state doctrine, in 832. This was the capital mistake, because all disbelievers were then committing a capital crime which carried severe punishment, mostly death.

The Koran, at this time, was not only questioned but ridiculed. The Islamic philosopher Al-Kindi, born 803, was part of the Mutazilites but changed sides early enough to miss martyrdom. In short: orthodox Islam was about to collapse - as it is today, mind you!

Three factors saved it at that crucial time:

- first, a conservative Caliph, Al-Mutawakkil

- secondly, the Turkish palace guard who had shortly before converted to Islam and had no stomach for having the Koran diluted

- thirdly, as in all ages, the ingrained belief of the uneducated people which is clinging to the proven instruments of consolation and a better life thereafter.

In order to be brief, the pendulum swung sharply back. Now the Mutazilites were persecuted with the same holy furor that has been the trademark of pogroms, inquisition and holocausts ever since - and also before.

The Shia sect was forbidden, Jews and Christians were reduced to citizens second class. The yellow star of David which I still saw on the Jews of Nazi Germany had its roots directly there.

(W): I am jumping, much to my misery, now over the Mutakallimun i.e. logicians, who raised their voice around the year of 900, to reconcile Islamic dogma with Greek philosophy, which made them the scholastics of Islam, long before Maimonides came in the 12th century to try this again for Judaism or Thomas Aquinas who in the 13th century tried to put christian doctrine into the Procrustes bed of his homophile Aristotle.

To come to an end: The Islamic faith has had no reformation until now. Orthodox Islam is still demanding a literal belief in the Koran. Full stop. They really think that the present world, with all its evolutionary process, can be explained by Koran and Hadith. The trouble is: if not so, then not the Koran, but the world has to change! And now we are in the middle of dynamite!

B: When you were talking, I was a little bit worried if you would have a safe landing. Thank you for the overview, it was essential, this I understand now. But where do we go on from here?

W: For one thing, we have Mutazilites again and they are persecuted today with the same unforgiving zeal for which Islam is famous. Take Mr. Nasr Hamid Abud Zaid, professor, of Egypt, to whom the fundamentalists contested his lawful marriage to his wife of more than 20 years, as he went public with his views. He is living in exile now in Germany. Take the terror which Ms. Tamila Nasreen of Bangla Desh is exposed to. Or Mr. Salman Rushdie. His „Satanic Verses" I do not like personally. But apparently the orthodox leaders are of the opinion that they have a deity which can be insulted, and, still worse: feels insulted.

Here, in the strict adherence to the letter of the Koran, is the first fault line which is very fast turning into a Rift Valley of Islam:
They bungled the chance for a Reformation one thousand years ago and now, in our days, the issue cannot be avoided any more, which means that every Moslem will have to decide whether the Koran - and the Hadith all the more - can be interpreted also in an allegoric way. Since we cannot expect that more than half of all Muslimin will share this view, there will be bloodshed. The rest of the world, condemned as „devilish" anyway by the orthodox, will not be called upon to settle the issue.

B: It´s scary, because it has started already. But have you ever imagined that you are putting the same decision before a believer in the four reports on Yeshua? That they can be interpreted also allegorically - and that means at the will of every believer, whatever his/her education and grasp may be?

W: Of course I see the parallel. But there is one fundamental difference in the revelation of the two religions. The Logos from Yeshua made no compromises and claimed existence before all time. We have declared him to be not omniscient in our past chapter. But still, he/she/it looms far over any revelation that became to a Mohammad. And on the whole: compared to Yeshua his teachings are mostly a repetition of Judaism and the four reports - with all due respect.

B: So you are putting the revelation through Yeshua over the enlightenment of Mohammad?

W: Certainly I do. Enlightened? Very probably so, especially if the Divine Spirit saw the fiasco of the so-called christian beliefs 700 years after the demise of Yeshua.

B: You are still owing me the second load of dynamite in Islam?

W: One would be more than enough, but there really is the second. Islam was always connected to a feudal system, just as the so-called Old Testament and the four reports on Yeshua. The surprising fact is that this concept worked flawlessly over the centuries, and still does today in many parts of the world. To the prince/king went all the revenues of the state, be it incense or oil. The Royal Treasury saw very carefully to the prescriptions of the Koran. Looking today at the Emirates or Saudi Arabia we have to say with respect that people were never better cared for than in this system.

What the feudal concept of Islam wanted, and realized over the centuries, is the welfare of the subjects. As long as their systems were feudal Islam worked to perfection, because the prince/king saw to it that Islamic faith was practised. I dare to say that in no other social system of this planet a better solution was invented. And, mind you, it is still being practised.

B: All right, granted. But where is the worm in the apple?

W: Not in the feudal systems. They operate to satisfaction and it is only to the second university semestre minds who demand that they have to be abolished.

B: I do not want this general answer. Where is the worm in the apple of Islam? Or rather: the second worm?

W: The term „worm" I do not like at all, my friend. When we were talking about dynamite earlier it was to tear open the vista to a spiritual event which is going to claim its place after some 1.000 years.

But when we are talking about the situation of Islam in non-feudal states, in so-called „democratic" states, then we are in for real trouble.

B: The way you are pronouncing „democratic" it means to me that these states are anything but democratic?

W: You are right on target. Just take the examples of Pakistan, Malaysia, Myanmar, Indonesia, Algeria or Egypt. They can present a foreground of democratic alibis. In essence they are the reign of „holy families"; you can include all India very nicely in this fold. Or, they are simply the army, where generals want to get rich before retirement. Or they are „consultants" to this and that.

And then comes the family interest. I do not have to delve into the greasy connections of the Suharto family in order to be understood.

B: Thank you, I understood this already before your presentation. But where is the second load of dynamite?

W: You experience it already in Algeria and Egypt. Other Islamic countries have not yet come to the point of despair, where they only see terror as the instrument of change.

The line of reasoning there is, very much simplified, the following: One third of the labor force is not able to get a job, since years. Education and health are for the rich only. Adolescents have no perspective. The cooking pot stays cold. The infant death rate is staggering. On the other hand we see flagrant corruption in the public administration, the amassing of wealth in the hands of a joyful, healthy, saturated elite. Alms giving, yes, perhaps in the subsidized price of bread - nothing more. Elections are rigged, government jobs go to the highest bidder. This never happened under the old princely rulers.

(W): These so-called democratic rulers are nothing but an economic oligarchy in power, plutocrats, just changing the sides of the feeding through periodically.

And, I am still quoting, the orthodox witness a laxity of morals especially by the obscene marketing of female beauty, heated by imported television, lurid magazines, cinemas. Adultery becomes rampant, child obedience is crumbling, and - in the end - the Koran is laughed at. The whole process could set in only because our princely rulers have been chased out and because Koran and Hadith count for nothing any more.

We cannot revive our feudal rulers, but we can revive the validity of the Koran - literally, please! And this is what we are doing now: we start to fight against a socially unjust, spiritually sordid and thoroughly corrupted world with the clean letter of the Koran - and a few thousand Kalashnikovs!

B: This was a fine nut-shell explanation of the situation, thank you! So the basic driving force of the fundamentalist movement is social injustice?

W: So I believe, but this alone would not bring about the dynamite. The explosive power lies in the parallel intention to give a shining example to the rest of the world what Islam can accomplish if only the Koran was followed literally. The world has to change, not the Holy Book.

B: But so far I cannot see the world-wide eruption which you paint as a gruesome mural?

W: As with any born-again movement the fanatics will lead the masses. They will denounce all other Islamic states of the world, especially secular states like Turkey, or enlightened feudal states like Morocco, Saudi Arabia and the Emirates, as traitors of Allah´s cause. The exchange of gibes will be followed by that of rockets. Expecially Saudi Arabia as the protector of the Holy Places of Islam will come under fire - literally. And, as you can imagine, the non-Islamic world will not watch from the sidelines but will interact; not so much because they take spiritual sides but because of their oil interests in that region. If they are not stepping in as a bloc, i.e. the United Nations, but start to fight proxy wars by their respective clientele, then the world may be in for „the mother of all battles", as Mr. Saddam Hussein would phrase it.

B: Not a very comforting scenario, is it? Do you think that there is an alternative?

W: Yes, if the non-Islamic world is recognizing the social disorder in the so-called democratic Muslim states, not putting the cronyism with corrupt presidents and the rest of the „holy families" in the foreground, but by insisting on - and controlling them tersely - the necessary measures in land reform, health, food production, education - and so on. And, mind you, with a due respect for their version of Islam, if it is not exercised militantly or is in contrast to humanitarian law.

B: Are you daring to put a time tag on this development?

W: We have entered the explosive stage already. If the necessary reforms in the so-called democratic Islamic states are not happening within 10-20 years then the fundamentalists are trying to export their order to suffering brethren countries.

B: And why are you shying away from putting a time tag on the positive development?

W: You mean what time could pass by until the evolutionary forces in Islam can raise their heads again? Hard to say. In any case they will be able to do so only if a fratricidal war among the Muslimin can be avoided. Because even as the „enlightened" side would win, which we hope for in this case, the other side has the martyrs. After such an eruption you can say goodbye to evolution in t o t a l Islam for a string of centuries.

But if this worst-case scenario is not happening, then I foresee three to four generations. Why this? First because, the economic measures have to grip; with prosperity for all comes, gradually, the „luxury" of philosophy. You cannot argue about items of faith with a hungry, jobless and sick youth of 20 years, can you?

B: So we come to the notion that evolution of consciousness needs economic prosperity first?

W: Let me embrace you! I think that you just stated fact a fundamental law, or anything next to it! Also your ideas about a periodic spiritual chaos fit in nicely here; we shall discuss it in the following chapter.

(W): We have agreed earlier in this book that evolution happens in stages, plateaus. Pre-empting our next chapter I maintain that a progress in the evolution of the mind, consciousness, and a very directed one in our opinion, does not spring ready-made from a turbulent phase of new orientation - chaos, if you want so - but is moving in almost imperceptible steps within a calmed-down beneficial „climate" of economic development.

Mutations are not ripping the plateau apart, but are pervading it in myriads of ways, but they need a stable surrounding. So if we exchange the term „prosperity" which you used, by „sufficient belly food, peace and time to experiment - say thinking -" then we are in beautiful unison with the basic needs of evolution.

B: Quite a nice comparison, but I give it to you more cheaply: you cannot preach to somebody who is in a hurry or who is hungry. That´s the essence of it. Coming back to my question: how long for the positive alternative?

W: As of today, a minimum of five generations before the new Mutazilites have convinced the rest of Islam that the Koran is, by all means, subject to interpretation and allegoric reasoning without loosing one ounce of its splendour.

To this I say: so God is willing - Insch´allah!

B: Let me add: There is only one God, and God is great! Far greater than the so-called christian beliefs or the orthodox Muslimin think, or dare to think today.

Chaos Desired ?

B: Before we are entering into the discussion of a possible chaos phase after the demise of the priest churches we should clean this word of its negative taste. In everyday´s language chaos does not only mean the absence of controllable sequences or structures, but we are instantly also passing a moral verdict on it, that of disorder, unreliability, unsolidity, danger, catastrophe. Some anxious minds are even of the opinion that chaos is the direct source of Evil, disorder raised to a cosmic principle, which of course it is not.

W: Our children have received a better education than we did. One of these days I had a long discussion with my son on the concept of chaos and found that I had to do quite some homework before Mandelbrot figures, fractals or strange attractors meant something to me.

B: Chaos research is in its infancy still. Until today we have not made much progress over Democrit who postulated that it is only our unability to register and explain a great number of fast events in a non-linear way, i.e. not according to the principle of cause and effect.

Just take our human liver as an example. You smile, but it is a very fitting model. The more than 100.000 enzymatic reactions which take place there every second are happening in a chaotic milieu - „unseen" by our reason. But you have to admit that it works highly effectively. Therefore I did not smile for a moment when I read years ago that a Spanish doctor set up a marble memorial for the human liver with the argument that this organ is by far more intelligent than he, the whole man. The papers carried the picture world-wide.

W: We have to approach our central point. We agree with Democrit that there is no chaos but only our unability to predict definite events or to influence them. So „chaos" is more or less our resignation, the admitted inability of a still retarded consciousness. Agreed?

B: Yes. From there we come right into the mainline of this section: Do you think that it is not only possible, but highly necessary that the spread of the revelation by the Divine Spirit on this planet should undergo a chaotic phase? A phase, after which it will shine on a higher plateau of consciousness, and a much wider one?

W: Why wider?

B: Because it will reach many more people, believers, than ever before.

W: I give this development a high degree of probability to succeed, and it has started already. Depending on the side you take, e.g. that of the prelates, you are seeing dikes crumble under the onslaught of the waves of Evil, but their churches sitting squarely high on the rocks, unperturbed, while the gates of hell pound at their foundations.

If you take the view of millions, however, who are deeply satisfied to see the old order crumble because it became a perversion of the revelation, who will be able for the first time to take a deep breath of evolution, for them the battering waves cannot be high enough, they wish for a tsunami!

B: The comparison with a seaquake wave was not bad, but evolution never destroys.

W: All right, I was carried away with enthusiasm. But if we are looking for a short concept for the chaos phase I would call it foremost a hygienic phase for consciousness, a self-cleaning phase, catharsis.

B: Don´t you think that it will be possible - or desirable - that the priest churches of this world could develop new structures, but quickly, which might channel the waters into more quiet beds again. In other words: no chaos?

W: I fervently hope that this will not be the case. If you look back into history you observe that organisations that are replacing old orders after a catharsis are an unholy mixture of true former revolutionaries, but also of opportunists, deserters and soldiers of fortune, or very „political" minds - best regards from Talleyrand and Fouché! And in a moment you are having again, therefore, the old power conus again only in a different garb. No. This must not happen.

All this would be only an effort to harness the evolutionary minds, and to bring them back to „order" - their old order. You may take the example of harnessing periodical inundations or wildwater. The engineers create a huge basin, hydrodam, where the waters can be amassed without bringing damage. And then the sluice gates will be opened by the engineers that just so much spills out which is beneficial to the landscape - their irrigation system.

B: I see your point. So the „engineers" have to go?

W: As soon as possible.

B: And you reap an inundated, devastated landscape instead. Will that be better?

W: You surprise me. So far it was you who advocated an evolutionary chaos, no?

B: I beg the liberty to change my views during a discussion. Right now I tend more to the desirability of a succession order, re-tooled from top to bottom.

W: I cannot spare you another water example. When the Nile was inundating Egypt every year since milleniums, their engineers developed an intricate system of watering and de-watering and secured a minimum of two good crops a year. But when they built the Assuan hydrodam the nutrients were held back - the fertility of the land is in danger. Are you following the parallel?

B: Very much so. What we need, therefore, is the de-centralized irrigation system?

W: What is really bringing about your sudden change of mind, my friend? Out with it!

B: Well, here it is: the onset even of a desired chaos will be probably accompanied by excesses between the true, orthodox believers and the evolutionary half - and not only in the so-called christian beliefs of today, but in all priest-run churches of the world. The silent - too long silent - majorities all of a sudden will have no priests, no sacraments, no moral theologians, no more consolation, no more access to heaven. Do you really think that they will take all this lying down? Never! They will rise in a holy war against the „god-less, church-less, faith-less" elements, which are, of course, only another incarnation of Evil again, in their view.

W: So you are afraid that civil wars will break out over it?

B: Quite sure, if the new forces try to shut down the priest churches by force. We discussed it already. And I am getting ever greater doubts that the new forces will really behave evolutionary - and not revolutionary. Who will be there to tell them: No, wait, just dry them out, not pry them out! There will be no moral, world-wide authority to whom they would listen.

W: Be honest, my friend. Is it not so that you are - innermost - afraid of the possibility that an evolutionary chaos could result in a new mixture of beliefs, syncretism, where the revelation through Yeshua is watered down?

B: No, I do not. For once, because I firmly believe in the divine origin of the revelation through Yeshua -

W: - so do the Muslimin for their belief, so do the Shinto faithful! -

B: - it is personal belief, for sure, nothing else. The second reason is that a belief in the revelation through Yeshua, which has gone through a tempering fire of tolerance and the abolishment of central command structures will be a great invitation to participate for the rest of the world.

W: Why?

B: Because we are having the evolutionary answers, the perspective has been re-drawn, priestly arrogance has been abolished, two thousand year old superfluous doctrines have been scrapped, and, most of all, because we are out to change the present world in all its humanitarian sectors, but thoroughly this time, overriding any political resistance, cutting across all beliefs or factions.

W: Are you willing to give a time evaluation?

B: For the alternative, where today´s existing priest churches are substituted by supreme lay power in their organizations - four to five generations.

W: And for the chaos scenario?

B: If it materializes, there will be a protracted agony of all the priest churches - a millenium, maybe?

W: We are the end of our discussion, are we?

B: Yes, I prefer to have it ended, otherwise we would go in circles. Besides, I am deeply worried now.

.... Or A New Irrigation System ?

W: This section has been written by me only and is unique therefore in this book of dialogue. After our last discussion Bert was in a brooding mood; it was impossible for me to extract him out of it. So after a few days I sat down and wrote the following lines with some grains of humor, not for publication, only to knock him out of his „chaos blues", as I called them.

Before going on I have to say that I lived and worked for some time in Uganda. I left no offspring there, but I sat down and wrote a diary entry of my spiritual offspring as he had written it 500 years from now, in the year of 2497 A.C.. Please hear him out:

„Kampala, March 1st 2497.

Have been to our pineapple contract farmers in the Mukono region today. This year´s yield will be less than 17% against our export contracts. Have to lease another 300 hectares in the Jinja region! How else can we maintain the Scandinavian market with the Chinese yapping on our heels?

Dropped in with Madame Archbishop in the evening. She likes me because she knows that one of my ancestors was the co-author of the small book „Stone Age of Faith" which apparently was quite a furor at his time. Well, he was a Mzungu, a pink Caucasian, I am nicely dark brown - blessed be my grandmothers of 500 years - all very stout catholic believers.

Madam Archishop takes delight in asking me when our world-wide priest-run church would finally collapse, as predicted by my ancestor as desirable and probable.

Mostly I shrug, but when other guests are around Madame does not tire to discuss this topic, also this evening. So I started:
„Madame, my great-great and so on grandfather may have thought that he was a very wise man. This may have been so, but he also was a great fool. He overlooked two things or treated them negligibly, where there should have been warnings to him from way back of history:
First of all, that believers in a faith wanted at all times to have symbols, rituals, fanfares, pomp and circumstance - and priests who do their thinking for them - sorry, Madame!

Apparently he held all these things in cold disdain and talked and wrote about a Divine Power which remained a nebulous quantity compared to Jesus Christ and Holy Mary.

Secondly: he was betting on the evolution of consciousness, same as we do, but he wanted her to do his will, that is to create a mopping-up operation after him for the following 500 years or so, with his desired results, of course. Well, evolution thumbed her nose at him. „Nobody is dictating my speed to me", she said, „and one thing more: don´t consider yourself so important. You are not!"

Madame usually breaks into a pearly laughter at this, and, turning to the guests, she likes to add: „Your ancestor Walter did not have enough trust in us. He simply could not imagine that we, the bishops, - of course only men at that time - would put an end to Popedom roughly 400 years ago.

Your ancestor thought we were stupid or yellow - or both. Well, we were not, just biding our time. When we had the African vote solidly behind us in the next council, we told the last Pope - he was German, by the way - in flawless Latin: pack up and leave, your office is abolished. There will be no successor.

At the same council of Reijkavik in 2105 we abolished the cardinals, the Jesuits, all monk orders, and the Holy See as a state, it was high time indeed. Since then the Vatican is officially what it had been inofficially all along before, and for centuries: one big museum. Since 2105 there were only national Catholic churches as ours here, where the believers are also the church management. By the way, I am up for re-election in 5 months. Do I have your vote?"

Mostly I add to this that my predecessor could have had no idea also of the council of Hawai in 2131 which made the bold decisions of lifting the vow of celibacy on the clergy, admitted women to the priesthood and demanded that the Church get rid of all saleable assets. (Which is probably the reason why the husband of Madame asked me for a small personal loan again this evening).

Yes, my dear historical Walter, how should you have had also a notion of the council of Murmansk in 2164, where we united with the Anglican, Greek and Russian churches, and, of all things, with the Lutheran ones, with autonomy in ritual but with a joint evolutionary belief. Only that way it was possible to contain the militant Islam in the late decades of that century.

Since then, we are a truly Catholic church - encompassing all who believe in the revelation through Yeshua. But no more central command, infallibility and worse things.

Dear precursor, it is late and we shall have opportunity enough in the next life to exchange comments. I grant you that under your timely conditions you and your friend Bert have thought fearlessly, but you succumbed to the spiritual vanity of presenting a stage manuscript to the following generations. Anyway, it was worth the try. Cheers!"

This was the tongue-in-cheek contribution by me - and it had the desired effect; Bert went into a sound laughter again. What I did not expect was that Bert insisted that this paper must go into our book, to which I objected. „Now don´t get conceited", Bert said, „this is the best contribution you ever made on our expedition!" I am still figuring out whether this was a compliment - or the opposite. Anyway, here it was.

The Joy Of Evolutionary Belief

W: Now that we are coming to the end of our little book, if somebody would ask you: why have you written it? What would you answer?

B: It would be hard to make this person believe that fame or the prospect of earning some side money to my pension were not the driving forces. Even harder to swallow would be my denial that neither I nor you ever intended to be missionaries for a new sect, probably number. 2.500 plus, which again would have an organization, hierarchy or any other of these godforsaken - literally - anti-evolutionary packagings.

W: Don´t you think that a much more sinister intention is inferred on us, that of creating an outwardly religious organization but which is covertly designed to become not „a" but „the" secular power instrument?

B: Like the so-called „Scientology Church"? I get sick in my stomach whenever I read about their goal and methods. They should better call themselves „Operation Brainwash Inc.". On the other hand: why are organizations like these coming out of their holes in our times, as never before? Because they try to benefit from the spiritual vacuum which the traditional religions have created since centuries. Formerly this was not felt so, at least not as acutely as in our times, because the so-called christian churches presented a stable, monolithic outside appearance. Since this is crumbling, cunning and zealous men see their chance. Where there is a carcass, the vultures are assembling - do you remember that line?

W: Indeed I do; it´s another text which gains an evolutionary perspective today.

B: But inspite of many not-so-thank-yous I still owe you my reason why I felt that we should write this book. In the last essence it is the sheer joy of having arrived, after decades of reading, discussing, thinking and - yes - praying, at a system that gives very satisfactory answers to the roots of our spiritual existence; of evolution, as science confirms it on a cosmic scale, and the interlocking grip which the revelation through Yeshua has with the „as built" status of our consciousness.

W: May I add: plus the grandiose and utterly comforting horizon of expectations in this combination of natural evolution, as proven, and that of the forthcoming stages, plausible and believable. Before this background the concept „supra-natural" looses its meaning, because the whole process is „natural", so are all sub-stages of it, whether we understand them or not.

B: To come back to earth, let us say that we are feeling very, very protected. Man-made evil is threatening us, and the rest of the world, for centuries to come. But we shall develop here, on this planet, the international power monopoly that will slowly but steadily wrest this power from single nations. The term „protected" I also meant in an altogether different sense. Since we feel ourselves imbedded in an evolutionary cosmic system, science plus the Creator´s revelation, we can hardly be a promising target for the anti-force to which we thought us up in the second chapter.

W: Unshakable?

B: Unshakable. But now I want to get at the reward side of our view: what is „evolutionary faith", as we are calling it? By what is it distinguished against the contemporary beliefs of man? Let us use the analyzing method again which was helpful to us so far, all right?

W: Fine, I start. Let us take first the spiritual side of the coin. Who believes as we do, he/she understands that we are not alone in the universe. The scientific proof of planets existing besides our´s is practically in. That means that we are not detached and helpless spectators as the Nobel laureate Jacques Monod wanted to see our species in this universe, but an integral part of a developing consciousness in the whole observable cosmos - and probably in the non-observable just as well. In the whole universe beings have appeared, are appearing, who have reflexive thinking and free will -

B: - and the revelation of the Divine Spirit happens in all habitats of the universe where this free will has developed‚will develop, by evolutionary necessity.

W: We have discarded any notion, therefore, that our species should be a preferred one over others in the creation.

B: We carry a deep respect for life in all its forms, because we know how long it took on this earth to develop, and against what odds.

W: Are you thinking of this also when you are eating your next filet mignon?

B: You cannot derail me here, my friend. And what do you think if you eat your next slice of bread? Also this grain plant had to die, is´nt it? Sure, I am not very happy about the twisted trail of evolution on our planet which, at one point, decided that survival for our species is based on the necessity to kill and eat other species. With this we are stuck until the end of our terrestrial life, and animals or plants are killed for our survival without any basic difference.

W: Touché. Now I go to the more demanding aspect of evolutionary belief. We know by the revelation through Yeshua that the next life is not to be had for nothing. Of course we can never „earn" it; this silly notion is responsible for mega-tons of manuscripts and seas of tears in the so-called christian churches in the past centuries. But we can make it easier for the Divine Power to accept us if we behave in an evolutionary way down here, no?

B: Would you give a few examples?

W: Since we feel so closely tied together by evolution with other ethnic entities, nations, or Amazonas tribes, we demand their right to live in prosperity and dignity. We are intolerant only to intolerance, and with a smashing iron fist at that.

B: Now you are in the middle of terrestrial politics. Do the evolutionary believers need a political homeland? Do they have to establish political parties all over the world, putting themselves up for elections and so on? Amassing wealth which cements political clout?

W: Are you still in your senses? This would be the near end of evolutionary thinking. But, just in case, we believe that after such a catastrophy the evolution of mind would sprout a plant elsewhere quickly - has it planted probably already.

So: No, my friend! It would be a fatal mistake if the evolutionary believers would found political parties. The simple reason is that the concept „evolutionary" never can be a political platform in itself. Whatever is debated on political levels, from village councils to the forum of the United Nations, does not necessarily have an evolution component, but mostly pragmatic, matter-of-fact, reasonable and yet controversial aspects. Some of them may have evolutionary loads, very much so, e.g. the ecology problems.

You have to realize that evolutionary aspects carry the ultimate weight in any discussion on human or terrestrial affairs. We certainly are far off the point where this is respected. But if you invoke evolution at any given trifle point you are slowly but surely whittling it down to a negligible quantity - one of thousand arguments.

No, therefore! If we want to bring evolution into the discussion of our terrestrial affairs, then this will have to be reserved to really fundamental world issues which are destined to sweep the conscience of man. But if so, then let´s do it with all the explosive potential it can muster.

B: Fine. But how will the „evolutionists" in the various political camps recognize each other? Because what you are saying means nothing less than the forming of case-to-case evolutionary coalitions high above, and with contempt to the political parties. No question that the representatives may lose their parliament or Senate seat over this because they are shunning faction discipline, right?

W: They will have no problem to recognize each other very early in their faction sessions or in open parliamentary debate. It is not necessary even that the word „evolutionary" is used in the whole process. The problems that are coming up are not peanuts issues, but call for the personal conscience of every elected member of any house. Stand up and be counted!

B: Apart from the political life, would it not be helpful if the evolutionary believers in everyday´s life could identify themselves to each other and also to the rest of the world?

W: How do you propose to do that?

B: Creating a logo for themselves that can be worn on the lapel of a suit or - even studded with diamonds, why not - on an evening gown?

W: Are you having an idea already?

B: Yes. Why not use the Greek letter „epsilon", which is „e", for evolution?

W: Nice idea, but not without danger to the bearer. If he/she carries it he/she proclaims that the evolutionary belief in the revelation through Yeshua is put by him/her above anything in crucial matters - political party, Town Council, PTA meetings, charitable organizations, private life - whatever.

B: Exactly this would be the signal. When it comes to crossroads, this sign will say: my evolutionary belief is marching triumphantly over churches, sects, organizations, political parties, politics, my floor whip in the House and over my President - I do not care. On the other hand you can be sure that I am not a dummy of any open or covert organization but that it is ME!

W: An attractive idea. What is your best estimate that such a non-organization, as I am tempted to call it, will come into the open?

B: There I am very optimistic. I think that we shall see the first logos in one year after this book hits the markets.

———————————

Epilog, for Nicodemus

B: During the 25 years of our discussions we came across many great men and women who were in search of enlightenment. There is hardly anybody among them about whom we know less than Nicodemus, the Hebrew, the member of the Sanhedrin. And yet hardly anybody else has left a deeper impression on us than he. Why?

W: Probably because we see ourselves in him, searching for the next plateau of understanding - and not finding it in the way we expect it because we are burdened down with the ballast of history and tradition.

B: Every time I read this chapter III in Yochanaan´s report I get worked up over the way how the Logos in Yeshua treated this man in the discussion; cold, cruel, devastating. And this in the presence of the reporter who had established the contact.

W: Perhaps Yeshua was irked over the fact that Nicodemus came to him in the protection of the night instead of meeting him openly in bright daylight?

B: I do not think that this was the reason. A meeting in public with him would have ruined Nicodemus instantly, of course, the expulsion from the High Council would have lasted less than a day. And Nicodemus, as we believe, was from a family of high reputation, but the family would have been ostracized mercilessly also.

No. The Logos got acrimonious when Nicodemus could not follow him in his explanation of the spiritual life that we can expect after we shed our body. To us, who we have progressed in evolution, a spiritual re-birth brings of course the same barriers of understanding, but not of believing. Nicodemus, however, had not the shadow of such a concept in which he could believe. This is remarkable, since a personal life after death had become a tenet of Hebrew belief long before him. Still I cannot understand why the Logos in Yeshua pointed him out as a hopeless imbecile - of course this word was not used.

W: I think that just at this moment the Logos in Yeshua was acutely aware again of what he was up against with our human race, not only with the Hebrews. As in several other occasions this bitterness and resignation broke out of him. What is remarkable, however, is that the Logos from Yeshua considered these things to be within the dawning of belief in a man with the serenity of Nicodemus - which was not the case, however.

B: The whole discussion will have lasted some hours, as we may well believe, and only a fragment of it was recorded. What is more, we may also believe that the reporter, Yochanaan, understood practically nothing of the exchanges, at least not at this time. He recorded how h e understood the conversation.

W: All this may be. In any case I feel a pang of tristesse when I read these lines. Never before nor after we were nearer to learn something decisive on the evolution of our consciousness and its transformation into the bodyless dimension. What a pity!

B: Nicodemus was neither stupid nor obstinate. He simply had no conceptual possibility to deal with consciousness, evolution, or transformation.

W: And yet the Logos in Yeshua accused him that he, Nicodemus, as a teacher of Israel, should very well know these facts. So this can be interpreted only along one of the alternatives we discussed in this book, the one which maintains that the revelation came indeed to the Hebrews fully and clearly, but was trampled under.

B: We could make guesses for hours, but we must close. On that evening, however, 2.000 years ago, everything ended in total fiasco. Nicodemus, whom we may well see in advanced age already, will have returned to his home very distraught and disappointed, because he still believed that the Divine Spirit spoke through Yeshua, and he went on to believe this. What hurt him - and us also - was the manner in which the Logos had dispatched him.

W: As a wise man, as he doubtlessly was, he foresaw the end of Yeshua the man, since Yeshua acted already in the self-fulfilling prophecy of his end, isn´t it?

B: Certainly he did. He defended him in the Synhedrium until the last minute. Probably he was singled out already by his colleagues as a covert believer in Yeshua and had to risk his expulsion any time. In spite of this he tried to stem himself against the tide - but there was no more chance.

W: After that we meet him once more only in the reports, when he came to the burial of Yeshua, bringing the traditional embalming materials. After that, however, he vanishes from history. We would have expected him, in our minds, to appear in the reports again when Yeshua´s followers began to preach openly, or when Peter was jailed - but nothing. Apparently he could or would not follow the idea of resurrection, transition, whatever.

B: When Yeshua was murdered he did not want to witness it. The whole revolting scenery was observed by the hate faction of the High Council only. Where was he?

W: As I see him, he was on his knees in his house and remonstrated with his deity, under tears.

B: I am seeing him often before my eyes, standing on the flat roof of his house, looking to the starlit sky and praying for enlightenment, or rather a quantum leap thereof - and I am sure he was heard. When his personality left the body some day or in some night and was transformed, his joy must have known no boundaries. Now he knew.

W: I know what makes this great man so loveable to us. As he did, so we are starting our search from a given plateau of evolution. But as he, so do we register very acutely and very soon the limits of our four-dimensional terrestrial existence. In spite of that we continue to look fearlessly back, up and ahead, trusting in the imperturbable evolution and the equally unchangeable love of the Divine Spirit.

You, me, the reader - we all are Nicodemus.

On the author

Bert Widman was born in 1934 in Bavaria/Southern Germany. He entered the banking profession and was active in development banking, general contracting and export consulting for some 40 years.

His professional life brought him into early contact with different cultures and religions. This prompted him to take up the study of cultural history and philosophy since three decades, a never-ending and rewarding task in his opinion.

Not belonging to any church or sect he believes in a Creative Spirit which used the man Yeshua as its intermittent mouthpiece. So-called christian churches and sects made - and are still making - a singular travesty of this revelation. Evolution is not allowed to enter, so they end their life cycle as any priest-run organizations have done since 5.000 terrestrial years.

Bert Widman's prime interest is to penetrate beyond their present burial stage. For him, evolution is a universal constant. This is why burnt-out faith organizations, formerly criminal and corrupt, will sink into the abyss of oblivion; not so the misused revelation, however. For her a massive evolutionary metamorphosis is just coming up over the horizon, Mr. Widman maintains.

The author is living in second marriage, has three grown children and four grandchildren and resides near Lake Chiemsee, Bavaria.

Books by Bert Widman :

The Stone Age Of Faith

An evolutionary farewell
to churches and sects.
In plain language.
ISBN 3-89811-204-7

W h y , P a u l ?

An evolutionary inquiry.
In plain language.
ISBN 3-89811-202-0

A h e a d O f T h e i r T i m e s

An evolutionary presentation
of eminent heretics.
In plain language.
ISBN 3-89811-203-9

GEORG LINGENBRINK GMBH & CO. PUBLISHERS

Hamburg Frankfurt